Endgame for the Euro

DOI: 10.1057/9781137371904

Other Palgrave Pivot titles

Carroll P. Kakel III: **The Holocaust as Colonial Genocide: Hitler's 'Indian Wars' in the 'Wild East'**

Laura Linker: **Lucretian Thought in Late Stuart England: Debates about the Nature of the Soul**

Nicholas Birns: **Barbarian Memory: The Legacy of Early Medieval History in Early Modern Literature**

Adam Graycar and Tim Prenzler: **Understanding and Preventing Corruption**

Michael J. Pisani: **Consumption, Informal Markets, and the Underground Economy: Hispanic Consumption in South Texas**

Joan Marques: **Courage in the Twenty-First Century**

Samuel Tobin: **Portable Play in Everyday Life: The Nintendo DS**

George P. Smith: **Palliative Care and End-of-Life Decisions**

Majia Holmer Nadesan: **Fukushima and the Privatization of Risk**

Ian I. Mitroff, Lindan B. Hill, and Can M. Alpaslan: **Rethinking the Education Mess: A Systems Approach to Education Reform**

G. Douglas Atkins: **T.S. Eliot, Lancelot Andrewes, and the Word: Intersections of Literature and Christianity**

Emmeline Taylor: **Surveillance Schools: Security, Discipline and Control in Contemporary Education**

Daniel J. Hill and Daniel Whistler: **The Right to Wear Religious Symbols**

Donald Kirk: **Okinawa and Jeju: Bases of Discontent**

Sara Hsu: **Lessons in Sustainable Development from China & Taiwan**

Paola Coletti: **Evidence for Public Policy Design: How to Learn from Best Practices**

Thomas Paul Bonfiglio: **Why Is English Literature? Language and Letters for the Twenty-First Century**

David D. Grafton, Joseph F. Duggan, and Jason Craige Harris (eds): **Christian-Muslim Relations in the Anglican and Lutheran Communions**

Anthony B. Pinn: **What Has the Black Church to Do with Public Life?**

Catherine Conybeare: **The Laughter of Sarah: Biblical Exegesis, Feminist Theory, and the Laughter of Delight**

Peter D. Blair: **Congress's Own Think Tank: Learning from the Legacy of the Office of Technology Assessment (1973–1995)**

Daniel Tröhler: **Pestalozzi and the Educationalization of the World**

Geraldine Vaughan: **The 'Local' Irish in the West of Scotland, 1851–1921**

Matthew Feldman: **Ezra Pound's Fascist Propaganda, 1935–45**

Albert N. Link and John T. Scott: **Bending the Arc of Innovation: Public Support of R&D in Small, Entrepreneurial Firms**

DOI: 10.1057/9781137371904

palgrave▸pivot

Endgame for the Euro: A Critical History

Bill Lucarelli

University of Western Sydney, Australia

palgrave macmillan

DOI: 10.1057/9781137371904

First published 2013 by
PALGRAVE MACMILLAN

Palgrave Macmillan in the UK is an imprint of Macmillan Publishers Limited, registered in England, company number 785998, of Houndmills, Basingstoke, Hampshire RG21 6XS.

Palgrave Macmillan in the US is a division of St Martin's Press LLC, 175 Fifth Avenue, New York, NY 10010.

Palgrave Macmillan is the global academic imprint of the above companies and has companies and representatives throughout the world.

Palgrave® and Macmillan® are registered trademarks in the United States, the United Kingdom, Europe and other countries

ISBN: 978-1-137-37191-1 EPUB
ISBN: 978-1-137-37190-4 PDF
ISBN: 978-1-137-37189-8 Hardback

This book is printed on paper suitable for recycling and made from fully managed and sustained forest sources. Logging, pulping and manufacturing processes are expected to conform to the environmental regulations of the country of origin.

A catalogue record for this book is available from the British Library.

A catalog record for this book is available from the Library of Congress.

www.palgrave.com/pivot

DOI: 10.1057/9781137371904

Contents

List of Illustrations

Figures

Tables

 DOI: 10.1057/9781137371904

DOI: 10.1057/9781137371904

Acknowledgements

This book is dedicated to the heterodox movement in economics. Most of the chapters were earlier versions of papers presented to various Society of Heterodox Economists (SHE) conferences. A shorter version of Chapters 3 and 4 was published as "European Monetary Union: A Neoliberal Trojan Horse?" (2004), *Contributions to Political Economy*, Vol.23, Oxford. Chapter 7 was the basis for an abridged version published as "German Neo-Mercantilism and the European Sovereign Debt Crisis" (2011–12), *Journal of Post Keynesian Economics*, Vol.34, No.2. Chapter 8 was published as "The Break-Up of the Eurozone?" (2012), *The Economic and Labour Relations Review*, Vol.23, No.4.

DOI: 10.1057/9781137371904

List of Abbreviations

BIS	Bank for International Settlements
CAP	Common Agricultural Policy
CDS	credit default swap
CET	Common External Tariff
DI	Divergence Indicator
DM	Deutsche Mark
EC	European Community
ECB	European Central Bank
ECOFIN	Council of Economic and Finance Ministers
ECSC	European Coal and Steel Community
ECU	European Currency Unit
EEC	European Economic Community
EFSF	European Financial Stability Fund
EFSM	European Financial Stabilization Mechanism
EFTA	European Free Trade Association
EIB	European Investment Bank
EMCF	European Monetary Co-operation Fund
EMI	European Monetary Institute
EMS	European Monetary System
EMU	European Monetary Union
EP	European Parliament
EPC	European Political Co-operation
ERDF	European Regional Development Fund
ERM	Exchange Rate Mechanism
ESCB	European System of Central Banks
ESM	European Stability Mechanism
ETUC	European Trade Union Confederation
EU	European Union
ICU	International Clearing Union

IMF	International Monetary Fund
IMP	Integrated Mediterranean Programme
MDS	maximum divergence spread
NATO	North Atlantic Treaty Organisation
NCB	national central bank
OCA	optimum currency area
OECD	Organisation of Economic Co-operation and Development
OPEC	Organisation of Petroleum Exporting Countries
PPP	purchasing power parity
REER	real effective exchange rate
SDR	Special Drawing Rights
SEA	Single European Act
SGP	Stability and Growth Pact
SPV	Special Purpose Vehicle
TARGET-2	Trans-European Automated Real Time Gross Settlement Express Transfer System
VSTF	Very Short-Term Financing Facility

DOI: 10.1057/9781137371904

Introduction

Lucarelli, Bill. *Endgame for the Euro: A Critical History.* Basingtoke: Palgrave Macmillan, 2013.
DOI: 10.1057/9781137371904.

The aim of this short volume is to provide a critical historical narrative of the evolution of the European Monetary Union (EMU). The current debt crisis that has engulfed the eurozone has its origins in the three-decade long struggle to create a zone of "monetary stability" in the wake of the demise of the international post-war Bretton Woods system in the early 1970s. The history of the EMU, culminating in the Maastricht blueprint in 1992, reveals that this deeply flawed monetary edifice was informed by the prevailing neoliberal/monetarist economic doctrines, favoured by Germany. These ideological preferences in the framing of EMU were deeply imbedded from the earliest experiments in the early 1970s. The final blueprint, embodied by the Maastricht design of the euro, witnessed the birth of an international currency that was devoid of a coherent sovereign power. As Eichengreen has quite succinctly argued, "But most fundamentally, the problem is that the euro is a currency without a state. It is the first major currency not backed by a major government, there being no euro-area government, only governments of the participating countries" (Eichengreen, 2011, p 130). A stateless currency is, indeed, akin to Pirandello's character in search of an author.

This study also intends to be a contribution to the critique of the existing economic theories that continue to inform the evolution of the euro. In the absence of a political union and a corresponding fiscal framework, the survival of the euro remains problematic. At the time of writing, the first act in this unfolding drama, or perhaps tragi-comedy, is being played out as millions of workers are thrown into the ranks of the unemployed, while the very foundations of the post-war "social market" economy are being systematically dismantled with the imposition of harsh, neoliberal austerity measures by the IMF/EU/ECB (Troika) on Europe's peripheral, deficit countries. These self-defeating policies threaten the very existence of the eurozone in its present form and have set in motion powerful centrifugal forces, which could ultimately derail the entire post-war European project.

In writing the history of the EMU, it is possible to diagnose the causes of its present dysfunction. But the benefit of hindsight is always fraught with ideological pre-conceptions. The real problem is to diagnose the underlying structural contradictions rather than the surface symptoms. It is necessary to develop an immanent critique of prevailing economic theories in order to reveal that these doctrines were themselves part of the longstanding problems that governed the institutional design of the euro-system. If these economic theories continue to inform the political discourse, then history will merely repeat itself with more tragic consequences. To be sure, the study of economics is inextricably bound up in the dominant ideology of an era. To paraphrase Marx, "The ruling ideology of an era is also the ideology of

DOI: 10.1057/9781137371904

the ruling class". Unlike the more exact natural sciences, economics remains the prisoner of ideology. Contrary to the positivistic claims of neoclassical theory, economics is governed by politics. In the words of E.H. Carr, "The science of economics presupposes a given political order and cannot be profitably studied in isolation from politics" (Carr, 1951, p.17).

Europe's present malaise reflects the fundamental incompatibility between the existence of a system of sovereign states, on the one hand, and the failure to develop corresponding state structures and institutions on the supranational level, on the other. This national/supranational dichotomy prevents the euro from acquiring the backing of a sovereign power. Political union would create a more coherent sovereign power to support a single currency. Quite contrary to monetarist theories of money, it will be argued that modern economies are characterised by the pre-eminence of chartalist forms of money. The government ultimately defines the nature of money by choosing the monetary unit that it will accept in the payment of taxes. Consequently, the issuing of fiat money implies that in order to pay taxes, economic agents need to acquire money. A monetary circuit is set in motion in which the money issued by the government presupposes that it is bestowed with the privileges of seigniorage. As the monopoly supplier of the currency, the state can set the price of those assets it is willing to buy since this is the only means by which civil society is compelled to pay taxes (Wray, 1998, p.7). But taxes can only be levied in the future insofar as the initial expenditures of firms and the state constitute the monetary circuit by which the final payment of taxes is realised. The central bank therefore creates credit by issuing debts onto itself in order to activate the spending of the government. The causation runs from the issuing of sovereign debt, which then allows governments to specify the amount of debts that the state needs to collect through taxation. This, in turn, will liquidate the debt obligations incurred by the state (or the Treasury) to the central bank (Parguez and Seccarella, 2000, p.111). Tax revenue simultaneously cancels the central bank debt, which has been issued in the original monetary circuit. In the chartalist conception, money is the ultimate creature of the state.

According to Smithin: "From this perspective, money is predominantly state money and the liabilities of the state central banks, for example, acquire the status of *valuata* or base money because of the coercive power of the state and, in particular, because of its ability to levy taxes on its citizens payable in its own currency" (2003, p.26). Government spending is therefore financed through the creation of fiat money, rather than through tax revenues or the issuing of bonds. In this context, bond sales are simply a means by which

DOI: 10.1057/9781137371904

excess reserves are sterilised in order to ensure a positive rate of interest in the central bank overnight or prime rate. Bond sales should rarely be used to finance government deficits, except in very exceptional cases of war and other crises. It follows that a balanced budget over the economic cycle represents the theoretical minimum that governments should aim to aspire. Indeed, there is a very sound argument, based upon the tenets of functional finance, that moderate budget deficits are required to maintain the issuing of government bonds and by so doing, provide the very rationale for the existence of a bond market. As Wray contends: "Budget deficits do not require 'borrowing' by the government (bond sales); rather, the government provides bonds to allow the public to hold interest-bearing alternatives to non-interest-bearing government money" (1998, p.19). At the same time, since commercial bank debts are convertible into fiat money, commercial banks are able to acquire central bank liabilities. Thus, a considerable proportion of state money circulates as commercial banknotes, which will appear as either assets or reserves on commercial bank balance sheets. Conversely, there is a certain amount of commercial bank money that circulates and is converted into fiat money as private economic agents, depending upon their liquidity preferences, choose to hold a proportion of these banknotes as cash. The extent to which commercial debts are regulated is determined by the central bank, which regulates the creation of liquidity. In the final analysis, credit money cannot exist without the state and all credit money is necessarily state money regardless of its form of circulation as either commercial credit or as central bank liabilities.

Given the inherent instability of financial markets and the historical recurrence of financial crises, central banks evolved to act as lenders of last resort. Indeed, central banks were originally created to provide purchasing power to the state. As the sole monopoly supplier of legal tender, the state would issue debt to the central bank and the central bank was legally inscribed with the privileges of issuing the official reserves. This allowed the central bank to preside over the regulation of private banknotes and was given the power to impose restrictions in the issuing of these banknotes by private banks. Private notes were soon replaced by central bank reserves as a means of payments in the settlement of inter-bank liabilities. In other words, central banknotes replaced commodity money as the numeraire into which private notes would be convertible (Wray, 1996, p.456). Central bank reserves now acted as the universal equivalent and central banks have been empowered with the ability to regulate the creation of private banknotes through the interest rate discount mechanism. In order to avoid

DOI: 10.1057/9781137371904

and mitigate the effects of a liquidation crisis, credit money is convertible into fiat money, which in theory can be issued without limit. As lender of last resort, the central bank is able to inject liquidity into the system in the short run to avert a credit crunch. According to Wray:

> Thus, a pyramidal structure has gradually evolved in which non-bank money is guaranteed by banks, is made convertible into bank money, and is retired issuing bank money; while bank money is guaranteed by the central bank, is made convertible into central bank money, and is retired issuing central bank money. (1998, p.256)

From a chartalist perspective, a "stateless" money appears to be an oxymoron. The lack of a coherent sovereign power to back the issuing of the euro can be explained to some extent by the post-war evolution of European institutions and agreements. The endogenous development of European capitalism since the war has been characterised by a peculiar dialectic between the imperatives of domestic accumulation mediated by the existing national states, on the one hand, and the objective necessity to furnish coherent supranational forms of state intervention and regulation in order to enlarge the territorial sphere of accumulation, on the other hand. This dialectic appears to be governed by both the historical terrain upon which European capitalism emerged after the war and by the logic of oligopolistic competition with their international rivals. Yet this simple national/supranational dichotomy has also been complicated by the very limits imposed by the neoliberal strategy, which has failed to establish parallel and dominant state regimes of governance on the supranational level. The crisis of European capitalism is at one and at the same time a political crisis of existing state forms of mediation and hegemony. The whole process of integration has been informed by neoliberal economic doctrines, which stress the ostensible economic virtues of national deregulation, the liberalisation of intra-European trade and the promotion of greater labour mobility across national frontiers but within an enlarged European "social space". After the creation of a customs union, the second stage of economic integration involved closer macroeconomic co-ordination between the national economies and the realisation of complete monetary union. Monetary union thus represents the highest stage in the construction of this economic edifice. A single currency would symbolise that economic convergence has now reached a stage in which political unification is possible. The euro, however, remains a stateless currency devoid of a coherent sovereign power. As Cohen argues:

DOI: 10.1057/9781137371904

> The euro is a currency without a country – the product of an international agreement, not the expression of a single sovereign power. Its success, therefore, is critically dependent on the continued co-operation of EMU's member states, which can hardly be guaranteed for all time. ... Decentralised decision-making among sovereign governments without some form of co-ordination is potentially a recipe for disaster. (2011, p.103)

Since the official launch of the euro in 2002, its role as a means of payments, reserve asset and unit of account in international transactions has been quite limited. The US dollar continues to reign supreme as the pre-eminent international currency. Quite simply, the euro cannot be considered a serious rival to the US dollar in the foreseeable future. Indeed, the current crisis could threaten the very survival of the euro. In 2010, the euro accounted for 30 per cent of all foreign exchange market turn-over and about 31 per cent of all global bond issues (Eichengreen, 2011, p.130). According to IMF data, the euro represented about 26 per cent of international foreign exchange reserves in 2007, increasing its share from 18 per cent in 1999. By contrast, the US dollar's share as an international reserve asset fell from 71 per cent to 63.8 per cent over the same period. The evidence suggests that central banks, sovereign states and the private money markets were reluctant to diversify away from the US dollar (Dyson, 2008b, p.16). As a means of payments and unit of account in international transactions, the US dollar has maintained its dominant role, accounting for over 85 per cent of the share in the volume of international trade and financial markets combined (Fields and Vernengo, 2012, p.11). The internationalisation of the euro has been confined to countries within the enlarged European Union and in the extra-peripheral states in the near East and in sub-Saharan Africa.

By virtue of its dominant status of incumbency and its extended international networks, which are maintained by highly liquid financial markets, the US dollar continues to be unrivalled as a reserve asset, means of payments and unit of account in international transactions. Since most US debt is denominated in US dollars and most US foreign assets are denominated in foreign currencies, the US' net international investment position tends to increase in the event of an effective exchange rate depreciation. At the same time, Wall Street acts as an international financial intermediary and enjoys relatively higher returns on its foreign investment than foreigners earn on their respective US investments. The US therefore continues to derive a profitable stream of income from its foreign assets which, to a large degree, compensates for its net liabilities abroad (Iley and Lewis, 2007, pp.147–48). Even though the US is a net creditor in relation to foreign direct investment and the ownership of equities abroad, this is more than offset by its

DOI: 10.1057/9781137371904

net liability position in the more interest-sensitive debt markets. The bias towards the holding of debt and interest-bearing assets by foreigners reinforces the seigniorage privileges enjoyed by US financial markets and the dominant role performed by the US dollar. In short, unlike the rest of the capitalist world, the US is capable of borrowing abroad in its own currency. The risk of a dollar depreciation is incurred almost entirely by the foreign holders of US dollar denominated assets. The extent to which the US can sustain this apparent enigma will ultimately depend upon the willingness of its international capitalist rivals to continue to finance the US current account deficits and the burgeoning foreign debt.

The continued resilience of the US dollar ultimately depends upon the US role as "world banker." As long as the US financial system can continue to intermediate and recycle the surpluses generated in East Asia and the oil-exporting countries, the pre-eminent role of the dollar as the principal means of international payments is preserved. At the same time, private capital inflows have acted as a "safety valve" or "shock absorber" in the event of a reverse flow of highly liquid capital from the indebted emerging markets of the periphery. In this case, the US dollar performs the role as the major reserve asset and provides a safe haven for speculative capital flights. In other words, the mechanism of dollar recycling ultimately reinforces US dollar hegemony in the event of a capital flight, which restores the role of the US dollar as the most important international store of value. According to Vasudevan:

> The US has played the role of the banker to the world, drawing in surpluses from Asia and the oil-exporting countries, and recycling these in the form of private capital flows to emerging markets in the periphery. The countercyclical pattern of the private flows to emerging markets was critical to the mechanism by which the dollar's role was preserved. These private capital flows served as a safety mechanism, enabling the export of crisis to the debtor-periphery. (2009, p.27)

In stark contrast, the eurozone is devoid of a common Treasury and a common exchange rate policy. This straightjacket prevents the euro from enjoying the privileges of international seigniorage and severely limits the ability of member states to finance their respective fiscal deficits through the conventional methods of "functional finance" that the US Treasury is capable and willing to implement (Lerner, 1943). In other words, member states of the eurozone no longer possess a monopoly over the issuing of fiat money. The euro is essentially a foreign currency, which implies that national fiscal deficits cannot be monetised. Indeed,

DOI: 10.1057/9781137371904

these constraints were the intended outcome of the neoliberal theories that governed the evolution of the euro. Under the euro, member states are at the mercy of international bond markets. Informed by neoliberal/monetarist theories, the eurozone's monetary architecture imposes the discipline of international financial markets onto sovereign states to maintain "fiscal rectitude". Eurozone member states are therefore quite vulnerable to the vagaries of speculative flights of capital. Furthermore, the European Central Bank (ECB) is prohibited from acting as a lender of last resort to member states and cannot undertake the conventional operations of quantitative easing.

The lack of automatic fiscal transfers on the supranational level – analogous to the US system of federalism – which are capable of financing intra-eurozone fiscal imbalances through the operation of automatic stabilisers, has been a major source of instability and has contributed to the present sovereign debt crisis. The unwillingness of Germany and the surplus countries to finance the deficit countries has led to further demands for a more severe version of the notorious Stability and Growth Pact (SGP).[1] German neo-mercantilism is at the very epicentre of Europe's descent into a secular phase of competitive disinflation and the persistence of economic stagnation. Neo-mercantilist austerity and wage repression in Germany imparts a powerful disinflationary impulse throughout the eurozone. Since currency devaluations are ruled out under the single currency, the peripheral/deficit countries are compelled to adjust internally by adopting similar policies of austerity and wage repression. This self-reinforcing deflationary spiral resembles the worst features of the inter-war gold standard regime.

The constraints imposed on the ECB by the Maastricht Treaty have made it almost impossible for the ECB to implement a coherent and uniform set of monetary policies because of the continued existence of inflationary differentials across the eurozone. The imposition of a "one-size-fits-all" monetary policy by the ECB has merely accentuated these divergent trends between the low inflation and high inflation countries. The official interest rate, set by the ECB over the entire eurozone, has led to the high inflation countries experiencing a relatively low real rate of interest, which has encouraged excessive credit creation and induced asset price booms, most notably in real estate in the deficit countries of Ireland, Spain, Portugal and Greece. The divergences of real effective exchange rates within the eurozone caused by these inflationary differentials also erode the international competitiveness of the peripheral countries. The contrast between US monetary and

DOI: 10.1057/9781137371904

exchange rate policies and the straightjacket imposed in the eurozone by the ECB could not be more prescient. As Fields and Vernengo contend:

> By buying great quantities of Treasuries, the Fed not only keeps stable bond prices and low interest rates, but also provides assurances that Treasury bonds remain a secure asset. That allows the US Treasury to maintain high fiscal deficits on a sustainable basis. That is the exact opposite of what the ECB has done for the countries in the periphery of Europe. Countries in the currency union lose control of monetary policy and cannot depreciate the exchange rate. But a common currency setting also brings to an end the possibility for a single nation to run fiscal deficits since the sources of funding are either removed or subjected to supra-national control. (2012, p.12)

It can be surmised that the flawed design of the euro – informed by the prevailing neoliberal/monetarist doctrines of "sound finance" and monetary "neutrality" – have wreaked havoc on the peripheral/deficit countries. This dangerously self-reinforcing logic between speculative bond markets and the cascading, deflationary spiral imposed on those countries encountering severe debt crises, poses an existential threat to the entire eurozone. This logic is akin to the inter-war gold standard regime in which a powerful deflationary impetus eventually destroyed the existing international monetary system and triggered a whole series of competitive devaluations and the outbreak of trade wars. Economic autarky gave rise to the formation of currency blocs and led to the ascendancy of economic nationalism and its more extreme manifestations in the guise of fascism. In the wake of the most severe economic slump since the Great Depression, it appears that some of the lessons of that era would need to be revisited.

Note

1 The signing of the new "fiscal pact" by 25 out of the 27 EU member states in March 2012 reinforced Germany's insistence on strict limits to budget deficits. According to Cohen (2012, p.697): "At the heart of the compact is a new 'golden rule' limiting primary budget deficits (i.e., deficits before interest payments) to no more than 0.5 per cent of GDP over the full economic cycle. Fiscal outcomes are to be carefully monitored by the European Commission in Brussels; and unles voted down by a weighted majority, costly sanctions are mandated for governments that breach the old SGP's deficit limit of three per cent of GDP. Henceforth, German stability culture would be the official dogma of Europe."

DOI: 10.1057/9781137371904

1
Origins of the Single Currency

Abstract: *The European desire to establish a "zone of monetary stability" has its origins in the wake of the international turmoil that accompanied the collapse of the post-war Bretton Woods agreements and the ensuing dollar crises during 1968–73. It was in this historical context and the threat posed to the Common Agricultural Policy (CAP) by gyrating intra-EEC exchange rates that the earliest proposals were formulated to insulate the Common Market from the instability generated by the dollar crisis and US inflationary policies. Indeed, then French President Charles de Gaulle had been one of the most indefatigable critics of what was described as the "exorbitant" privileges of US dollar seigniorage. This chapter will examine these earlier proposals towards European Monetary Union and the divergent Franco-German strategies, which were reflected in the contending blueprints for EMU.*[1]

Lucarelli, Bill. *Endgame for the Euro: A Critical History.* Basingtoke: Palgrave Macmillan, 2013.
DOI: 10.1057/9781137371904.

The dollar crisis, 1968–73

The demise of the international monetary system under the aegis of the Bretton Woods agreements was a seminal event in the early experiments towards European Monetary Union. With the collapse of the fixed exchange rate system governed by gold/dollar convertibility, international confidence in the dollar evaporated, which hastened an international exchange rate crisis. In stark contrast to the dollar shortage of the early post-war years, the US dollar had flooded world markets by the late 1960s. This enormous expansion of international liquidity was accentuated by the permissive financing of the Vietnam War as the US Treasury resorted to the printing press (Block, 1977). It was the emergence of US balance of payments deficits, however, that ultimately caused a loss of confidence in the US dollar/gold convertibility regime. This flight from the dollar led to a serious drain on US gold reserves, which declined from an estimated $23bn in 1950 to about $12bn in 1967. At the same time, official and private foreign dollar holdings increased from $15.1bn in 1957 to $31.5bn in 1968 (Gilpin, 1975a, p.58). The culmination of the gold drain and the loss of confidence in gold-dollar convertibility induced an unprecedented rise in the demand and market price for gold that eventually led to the demise of post-war Bretton Woods agreements. US seigniorage of the dollar had been accepted by foreign economic agents as long as it fostered the expansion of international trade. Yet the cohesion and stability of the fixed exchange rate system was ultimately dependent upon the ability and willingness of US authorities to act as a world central banker. As soon as their liabilities in the issuing of US dollars were no longer regarded as "good as gold", the "solvency" of the US monetary authorities in their role as world bankers was imperilled (Guerrieri and Padoan, 1986). In short, the success of the system was too highly dependent upon the capacity and willingness of the US monetary authorities to defend gold/dollar convertibility.

The relative decline of American industrial productivity and international competitiveness during the post-war era contributed to the erosion of the US role as reserve currency nation. Close analogies with the demise of the gold standard under the aegis of *Pax Britannica* can be drawn. Just as the decline of Britain's relative economic power had prefigured the dissolution of the gold standard, so too the relative decline of US economic power undermined its role as international central banker under the Bretton Woods system. Between 1950 and 1971, US productivity

DOI: 10.1057/9781137371904

growth had fallen behind the European Economic Community (EEC) by 35 per cent and Japan by as much as 60 per cent. During the same period, average annual productivity growth in the US was estimated at only 1.7 per cent, compared to 4.5 per cent in the EEC and 10.6 per cent in Japan (Kaldor, 1978, p.64). After the demise of the Bretton Woods system, successive US governments pursued a policy of "benign neglect", which allowed the dollar to progressively devalue (Parboni, 1981). It was assumed that successive dollar devaluations would contribute to the restoration of US international competitiveness. Dollar devaluations, however, tended to impart inflationary impulses transmitted through the expansion of international liquidity.

Under the fixed exchange rate system, only one country can set its monetary and exchange rate policies independently of all other countries. In the monetary literature this is defined as the *N-th country* paradox. If one assumes that a group of countries are governed by a fixed exchange rate regime, only *country N* is theoretically able to fix its exchange rate in relation to countries *N–1*. The *N-th country* therefore performs an anchor role or reference point in an asymmetrical system to which all of the other countries are compelled to align themselves. Under the former Bretton Woods system, the US economy performed this dominant anchor role (Moon, 1982). In the monetary sphere, this privileged position manifests itself in the financial gains accrued through seigniorage. Despite the demise of the fixed exchange rate regime, the US dollar continued to perform the role of international means of payments and reserve asset. Indeed, the US was no longer constrained by its obligations to accumulate gold reserves in order to defend gold/dollar convertibility. It was now possible for the US monetary authorities to pursue reflationary policies and dollar devaluations in order to restore their international competitiveness (Parboni, 1981). The relatively small tradeable sector of the US economy as measured as a share of GDP implied that successive devaluations of the dollar were more inflationary overseas than within the domestic economy. The US economy was therefore capable of "exporting" inflation through an increase in international liquidity. Its major industrial rivals were more vulnerable to the inflationary consequences of US expansionary domestic policies.

In Western Europe, these inflationary US policies had an adverse impact, while the demise of the gold/dollar convertibility regime generated speculative capital flows and exchange rate instability. It was in this volatile environment that General de Gaulle demanded a return

DOI: 10.1057/9781137371904

to the gold standard. West Germany and Japan, however, were willing to finance the US balance of payments deficits in order to preserve the Western military alliance (Gilpin, 1975b, p.154). But as the dollar crisis intensified, exchange rate volatility within the Community threatened further progress towards closer economic union. Exchange rate convergence became necessary to prevent a general drift towards intra-EEC competitive devaluations and economic nationalism. The dollar crisis thus spurred European leaders to construct a zone of monetary stability across the Atlantic (Kruse, 1980).

The exponential growth of the private Eurodollar market was the most visible manifestation of this unregulated expansion of international liquidity and credit creation (Aglietta, 1982). After the demise of the gold/dollar regime, demand for liquidity increased as both international firms and central banks resorted to the Eurodollar market as a source of credit. The origins of this market can be traced back to the Kennedy administration in which the US Federal Reserve Bank had imposed limits on interest rates to deposits within the domestic economy (Kindleberger, 1984, p.445). With the restoration of currency convertibility in 1958, financial institutions in Europe could purchase US bonds and securities and engage in foreign exchange transactions. Since investors could earn a higher rate of return by transferring their funds from the US to the Eurodollar market, the growth of the latter was set in motion. The magnitude of this flight of capital was reflected in the expansion of US banks operating abroad; by 1972 there were 107 banks with total assets exceeding $80bn. Two years later, this figure had increased to an estimated $140bn or equivalent to one-fifth of the value of the US national product (Mayer, 1974, p.437). Most of the transactions of the Eurodollar market occurred in the London branches of US banks who would issue "certificates of deposits" against the payment of their dollar liabilities in the US. Since US banks retained possession of dollars deposited abroad, the growth of lending in US dollars by international financial agents generated a multiplier effect and increased the volume of international liquidity. The Eurodollar market therefore acted as a transmission mechanism in the expansion of international liquidity and contributed to the inflationary upsurge of the 1970s.

The "Triffin dilemma" as it became known essentially states that in order to supply the international economy with US dollars, the United States itself would be obliged to run burgeoning balance of payments deficits to avoid a drain on international liquidity. But the very growth of

DOI: 10.1057/9781137371904

these US deficits would ultimately undermine the international status of the US dollar and provoke a series of crises. This contradiction would set in motion cycles of expansion and contraction of international liquidity and generate systemic instability (Triffin, 1961). The continued benefits enjoyed by the US monetary authorities as a result of dollar seigniorage suggests that the US dollar continues to perform the pre-eminent role as an international means of payments and reserve asset. The "Triffin dilemma" was therefore writ large. In the post-Bretton Woods era of the floating dollar standard, the US financial system has evolved from being simply the issuer of the reserve currency to the principal issuer of interest-bearing, short-term liabilities to the rest of the world. Indeed, the existing international monetary system is quite unique because international "money" ceases to have a standard unit of value, analogous to the dollar/gold convertibility system or the nineteenth-century gold standard regime under the aegis of *Pax Britannica*. In the absence of an objective standard of value, currencies possess only "fiat" values, which are governed by future expectations under the guise of hedging and speculative operations performed by the foreign exchange and derivatives markets (Lucarelli, 2011). In the event of a credit crunch, the US dollar assumes its role as an international safe haven and reserve asset.

Consequently, the entire pyramid of credit was no longer governed by the regime of regulation based upon gold/dollar convertibility. A more laissez faire system had emerged governed by what was euphemistically described as the "paper dollar" standard. Despite the demise of the Bretton Woods system, the US balance of payments and domestic US interest rates continued to act as the unofficial pivot by which international liquidity was likely to behave. This dynamic depends quite critically on the continuation of the strategic role performed by the US dollar in international trade and payments. In the absence of the regulatory function performed by a fixed exchange rate regime, international liquidity is governed by the foreign exchange markets in derivatives and futures. The cessation of gold/dollar convertibility did not necessarily imply the demise of the strategic international role of the dollar. Indeed, the expansion of international liquidity had more than quadrupled in the decade after the collapse of the Bretton Woods system (Triffin, 1978, p.270). US trade deficits were no longer financed by the depletion of US gold reserves but by the acceptance of central banks of US Treasury bonds and debts in the form of international reserves. Unlike all other capitalist countries, the US economy was no longer burdened by a balance of

DOI: 10.1057/9781137371904

payments constraint. The US dollar continued to reign supreme as the world's foremost reserve currency, as the principal intervention currency by central banks and as the major numeraire in international transactions. The emergence of this free market system, however, bred speculation, exchange rate volatility and inter-state rivalry over markets and investment outlets. A relatively stable hegemonic regime was replaced by an oligopolistic system driven by competition and rivalry between the US, Japan and the EEC.

With the relative demise of *Pax Americana*, trans-Atlantic co-operation was increasingly eclipsed by rivalry and competition. This rivalry between the EEC and the United States over markets and investment outlets intensified in the wake of the dollar crisis, the onset of the severe recession of 1972–75 and the oil price shocks. It was in this volatile environment of exchange rate instability, an inflationary upsurge and the outbreak of financial speculation that eventually hastened European attempts to establish a zone of monetary stability. Exchange rate instability that generated speculative flows of "hot" money not only imperilled the Common Agricultural Policy but also threatened to undermine the entire process of European economic integration. The dollar crisis thus reverberated in the European corridors of power. According to an early proponent of EMU, "Only by creating a substitute for the dollar can Europe free itself from dependence on it, and only through this means can the US correct its balance of payments" (Mundell, 1973, p.125).

Proposals for a monetary union

Before the onset of the dollar crisis, the EEC had been preoccupied with the completion of the customs union and the CAP. Monetary issues were considered less urgent. Although the Treaty of Rome had not explicitly endorsed the objective of monetary union, it did propose closer co-ordination of national economic policies (Articles 103–108). After the restoration of currency convertibility in 1958, the European parliament had convened preliminary discussions exploring the issue of monetary union. Monnet's Action Committee had adopted the Triffin Plan, which involved the creation of a European monetary fund to counter short-term, speculative capital flights. Triffin's proposals had cast doubts over the survival of the Bretton Woods accords as early as 1961. At the time, however, these proposals appeared to be too ambitious

DOI: 10.1057/9781137371904

for the Commission, which had to contend with Gaullist opposition to federalist ideas. Despite these apparent difficulties, the Commission's Action Programme for the Second Stage of European Union had already stated its intention to focus on fiscal, monetary and exchange rate co-ordination. A Monetary Committee, represented by two delegates from each member state, was established to consult over the co-ordination of central bank policies, which was augmented by the monthly meetings of Central Bank Governors under the auspices of the Bank for International Settlements (BIS). The Commission also established the Medium Term Economic Policy Committee in April 1964 to enact five year plans. Informed by the methods of French indicative planning, the Committee would set out to promote common Community targets for economic growth and the gradual convergence of macroeconomic policies. Neither the Medium-Term Economic Committee, nor the Monetary Committee, however, could galvanise the necessary political consensus to promote these supranational objectives. National prerogatives continued to govern economic policy (Holland, 1975).

The post-war international payments system under the aegis of the Bretton Woods system had furnished a high degree of exchange rate stability. As the American economy expanded, it provided an engine of growth and an expanding export market for the OECD countries. As long as international economic growth and trade expansion continued unabated, the imperatives of EMU were less urgent. In only 18 months between 1967 and 1968, however, the international economy was thrown into turmoil by three major exchange rate crises: the liquidation of the pound/sterling regime in November 1967, the dollar crisis of March 1968 and the speculative attack on the French franc and German mark in November 1968. At the very epicentre of this financial meltdown was the demise of the fixed exchange rate system based on gold/dollar convertibility. After all attempts to stabilise gold prices had failed, a two-tiered system emerged in which the official price of gold was preserved at $35 per ounce between central banks but the market price was allowed to fluctuate. This system merely bred further speculation. In the meantime, multilateral negotiations had been convened by the Group of Ten industrial countries to devise a new means of issuing international reserves. An agreement was reached to create Special Drawing Rights (SDRs) issued by the International Monetary Fund and managed jointly by the Group of Ten (Spero, 1977, p.48). These proposals ultimately failed to prevent the collapse of the international monetary system. Indeed, the

DOI: 10.1057/9781137371904

failure to manage the crisis provided the political rationale for the EEC to devise its own plans for monetary union.

The initial catalyst appeared in France in early 1968. In May a general strike paralysed production for a month and provoked a financial panic as France's current account fell from a surplus of Ffr600mn to a deficit of over Ffr3bn by the end of the year. Accompanied by the dollar crisis, a general loss of confidence in the franc put pressure on the French authorities to devalue. At the same time, the German authorities experienced an enormous inflow of capital, which caused the exchange rate to appreciate quite sharply. Despite the overwhelming evidence in favour of an exchange rate re-alignment, both the French and German authorities refused to modify their respective parities. De Gaulle, in particular, had rejected devaluation because this would have been tantamount to a declaration of failure in the government's economic policies. A strong franc was perceived to be a powerful symbol of France's economic prestige (Eichengreen, 2011, p.73). Both governments resorted to the imposition of capital and exchange rate controls to prevent destabilising exchange rate fluctuations. Although these measures temporarily restored confidence, the underlying trade imbalance continued to deteriorate. After the resignation of de Gaulle in April 1969, the new government, led by Pompidou, finally succumbed to a devaluation of 11.1 per cent in August (Salvati, 1981, p.332). In the meantime, the newly elected Social Democratic government led by Chancellor Brandt in West Germany was obliged to float the mark in October.

Quite clearly, the exchange rate crisis of 1968–69 had exposed the limitations of existing methods of co-operation between Community central banks. It became evident that when confronted by the sheer size of the private Eurodollar market, national reserves were not sufficient to prevent exchange rate re-alignments and governments were eventually forced to make the necessary exchange rate adjustments. The Bundesbank had provided a credit line of over DM4.5bn to the French monetary authorities in 1968 to defend existing parities (Kruse, 1980, p.41). Despite these central bank swap agreements, both governments continued to be at the mercy of speculators. The process of adjustment was too cumbersome and dependent on political decisions, which would delay the appropriate response and breed further uncertainty. Short-term credit to deficit countries was neither automatic nor efficient. A more efficient mechanism was therefore required that would prevent delays and establish automatic credit lines. Furthermore, a Community

DOI: 10.1057/9781137371904

reserve fund would not only bolster reserves to defend exchange rates against speculative attacks, but could also provide the basis for a possible currency bloc to counter the gyrations of the US dollar.

The French government had blamed much of the crisis on US exchange rate and monetary policies. De Gaulle and his economics advisor, Jacques Rueff – who had coined the term "exorbitant privilege" to describe US dollar seigniorage – resented US private agents acquiring French assets with overvalued "paper" dollars. These perceptions were reinforced by the two Barre Plans, which sought to elevate the Community's monetary profile on the international stage. In this sense, the first Barre Plan in February 1969 represented the first coherent blueprint for EMU. The Report recommended that progress should be pursued in the co-ordination of macroeconomic policies and the creation of a mutual assistance fund to aid members in the event of an exchange rate crisis. Even though the Barre Report had rejected the creation of supranational institutions and a European central bank, it was still considered too interventionist by the German monetary authorities. The Bundesbank was quite reluctant to compromise its independence. After a series of intense negotiations, a few of the recommendations were adopted by the Council of Finance and Economic Ministers (ECOFIN) in January 1970. In the final agreement, proposals for closer co-ordination of short and medium term macroeconomic policies were adopted as well as the creation of a short-term credit facility endowed with a fund of 2 billion US dollars, which would be deployed against speculative attacks on national currencies.

Despite these concessions, the Barre Plan encountered strident West German opposition. As the principal creditors, the West German monetary authorities opposed any further increase in the credit facility to stabilise intra-Community exchange rates. Their greatest concern was the inflationary impact caused by the inflow of US dollars and were therefore very reluctant to allow the DM to become an international reserve currency. Indeed, the Bundesbank had imposed restrictions on the DM as an international means of payments and pursued a strategy of sterilising the inflow of capital to prevent excessive credit creation. The election of the Social Democratic-Liberal alliance in 1969, however, witnessed a reversal of Germany's former resistance to closer monetary union. Chancellor Brandt was an enthusiastic advocate of EMU as a means by which to preserve German export markets in Europe and as a defensive mechanism to counter the destabilising impact of dollar devaluations. Convened by the European Heads of State in December

DOI: 10.1057/9781137371904

1969, the Hague Summit provided Chancellor Brandt with the opportunity to promote the German proposals for EMU. The Hague Summit established a Committee, chaired by Pierre Werner of Luxembourg, to devise a strategy for EMU. Released in October 1970, the Werner Report recommended that monetary union should be accomplished over a ten-year time frame involving three progressive stages. In its final form, monetary union would exhibit the following attributes:

- A single currency achieved through the elimination of margins of fluctuation and the irrevocable fixing of exchange rates.
- The liberalisation of capital markets within the Community.
- The pooling of national reserves and the creation of a federal system of central banks.
- The centralisation of economic policies under the auspices of supranational institutions attached to the European Parliament and the Commission.

The first stage was scheduled over three years in which exchange rate movements would be narrowed within the agreed margins of fluctuation. This would be followed by the second stage over the next three years in which medium-term economic policies would be harmonised and a European Monetary Co-operation Fund (EMCF) would be established to co-ordinate central bank open market operations. The EMCF would gradually increase its supervisory powers over the agreed exchange rate margins of fluctuation. In the final stage, there would be the irrevocable locking of exchange rates and the EMCF would perform the technical functions of a European central bank and eventually issue a single currency. This would be accompanied by closer co-ordination of national fiscal policies and the liberalisation of capital markets. In order to promote a more balanced economic development, there would be a strengthening of structural and regional policies. In its more controversial recommendations, the Werner Report had proposed the creation of supranational institutions, which would eventually override national economic policies. Economic and monetary union thus implied further progress towards European political federation.

The implicit federalist elements of the Werner Report proved difficult to reconcile with both the French and German positions, while the issue of the transfer of executive powers would require a radical revision of the Rome Treaties. Differences over the types of strategy to adopt towards EMU had already emerged between the French and German representatives

DOI: 10.1057/9781137371904

during the Hague Summit. These diverging views were to crystallise into two major camps in subsequent negotiations. The "monetarists" were associated with representatives from France, Belgium and Luxembourg, most of whom advocated a rapid transition towards monetary union. The "economists", on the other hand, were represented by German and Dutch experts, who proposed a more gradualist approach which would involve closer economic convergence as a pre-condition to monetary union. In an attempt to reconcile these divergent views, the Werner Committee adopted a strategy of "parallelism" in which economic and monetary union would be pursued simultaneously. The overriding monetary objective, however, was unequivocal as page 5 of the Report states:

> A unified monetary zone implies the convertibility of currencies, the elimination of margins of fluctuations between parities and the complete freeing of capital movements. This can be achieved by keeping the existing national currencies or by establishing a common currency. Technically the choice would appear unimportant. However, psychological and political considerations would strongly support the adoption of a single currency thus generating the irreversibility of the action.

The most comprehensive statement of the "monetarist" case was expressed in the second Barre Plan in March 1970 (Appendix 1A). Unlike the Werner Plan, the pooling of national reserves and the creation of a European monetary fund would be achieved as part of the first stage. Furthermore, central bank interventions would be made in a European unit of account instead of the US dollar. The "monetarists" therefore sought to preserve national sovereignty over fiscal policies but project a unified monetary response to the rest of the world. The origins of the "economist" strategy can be identified with the Schiller Plan, submitted to the Council in February 1971. The West German Economics Minister proposed the realisation of economic and monetary union through four progressive stages involving the convergence of national macroeconomic policies with specific targets set for national inflation rates and interest rate differentials. In the final stage, a federal system of central banks would be established, which would issue a single currency modelled on the independent Charter of the Bundesbank (Appendix 1B).

At stake in these debates was the issue of which countries should incur the greatest burden of adjustment. While the Bundesbank was unwilling to surrender its virulent anti-inflationary stance in the event of monetary union, the French authorities were less willing to sacrifice their high rates of economic growth. These divisions doubtless reflected a more general

DOI: 10.1057/9781137371904

incompatibility between the economic policies of the two countries. The post-war German economic model had been inherently anti-Keynesian, relying instead on the "social-market" economy to stabilise the business cycle. This was in contrast to the Keynesian policies and economic planning of the French state which fostered an environment of relatively cheap credit to stimulate industrial development and the rapid expansion of domestic demand. The French authorities were thus more willing to tolerate higher inflation in order to achieve higher rates of economic growth and employment, whereas the German authorities adhered to a stringent anti-inflationary policy and a strategy of export-led growth (Hall, 1984, p.31). Although the French strategy of encouraging high rates of domestic growth was quite successful, it also induced recurrent balance of payments deficits and successive exchange rate devaluations. The Germans, on the other hand, experienced growing trade surpluses and the propensity for their exchange rate to appreciate. It was this fundamental incompatibility between the economic strategies of France and Germany that informed the debates over the issue of structural adjustment in the event of monetary union.

Conclusion

The emergence of the system of the floating dollar standard threatened to undermine the internal coherence of the EEC and its future progress towards greater economic integration. After the demise of the post-war Bretton Woods agreements in the early 1970s, the onset of extreme exchange rate volatility and the outbreak of speculative flights of short-term, highly mobile capital, set the stage for European attempts to establish a zone of monetary stability. These earlier proposals for EMU were quite seminal. In retrospect, the contending blueprints for a monetary union were to prefigure future proposals. Indeed, the basic elements of the Werner Plan re-emerged to inform the Delors Plan more than 20 years later. Similarly, the Schiller Plan advocated by German representatives reflected the anti-inflationary and anti-Keynesian ideological preferences of the Bundesbank. It can be surmised that the imperatives of German neo-mercantilism informed the German position. In this very real sense, the economist/monetarist divide was more an expression of conflicting national imperatives than a clash over competing economic theories. These divergent visions signified a more profound hegemonic struggle between France and Germany over the future design of the euro.

DOI: 10.1057/9781137371904

Appendix 1A: The second Barre plan (March 1970)

Stage one: 1970–71

- The provision of medium-term aid (using SDRs) and the adoption of a medium-term plan to co-ordinate economic policies.
- The harmonisation of credit policies under the supervision of central bank governors.
- The harmonisation of the VAT and the rules governing capital movements.

Stage two: 1972–75

- Economic objectives will be determined on the Community level but the creation of a European central bank is rejected.
- The margins of exchange rate fluctuations should be reduced to one per cent either side of parity.

Stage three: 1976–80

- The Council of Central Bank Governors to determine monetary policies.
- A European reserve fund established.
- The liberalisation of capital markets within the Community.
- The creation of a European unit of account as a means of settlement between central banks.

Appendix 1B: The Schiller plan (February 1971)

Stage one

- The co-ordination of macroeconomic policies in the short and medium terms.
- Short-term monetary targets established and the criteria for the convergence of national interest rates finalised.
- The creation of a short-term credit facility.

DOI: 10.1057/9781137371904

Stage two

- The promotion of a more balanced rate of economic growth through the convergence of national macroeconomic policies.
- A medium-term credit facility established to promote closer exchange rate alignments.

Stage three

- Community economic policies introduced to override national economic policy instruments.
- A federal reserve system of central banks established.
- An increase in medium-term financial aid to encourage structural adjustment in the less developed regions.
- The partial pooling of national reserves.

Stage four

The final stage would involve the transfer of monetary and exchange rate policy to a European central bank or a federal system of central banks. Exchange rates would be irrevocably fixed in order to establish the conditions for the issuing of a single European currency.

Note

1 European integration constitutes a political/institutional process. Its most enduring feature has been the Franco-German axis which, in varying degrees, still provides the central pivot around which the intra-Community bargaining process revolves. At the very heart of this post-war settlement was the desire of European leaders to avoid the possible revival of destructive inter-state rivalry and establish a more liberal economic order in the wake of the disastrous experience of economic depression and war.

DOI: 10.1057/9781137371904

2
EMU: The First Experiment

Abstract: *From the very outset, the European Common Market lacked the credibility that stems from having the attributes of an optimal currency zone. The EEC was devoid of these classical features of labour market mobility, fiscal transfer mechanisms and the synchronisation of national business cycles that characterise an optimal currency zone. Furthermore, economic divergences between the core and peripheral regions continued to generate centrifugal forces that threatened the internal cohesion of the EEC. Although the EEC failed to conform to the conditions necessary to establish an optimal currency area, the problem of asymmetrical shocks and the question of which countries would incur the main burden of adjustment in the event of monetary union, were to inform earlier experiments towards EMU. This chapter will examine the first experiment known as the "snake in the tunnel" and some of the theoretical problems associated with a system of fixed exchange rates.*

Lucarelli, Bill. *Endgame for the Euro: A Critical History.* Basingtoke: Palgrave Macmillan, 2013.
DOI: 10.1057/9781137371904.

 DOI: 10.1057/9781137371904

Introduction

From the very outset, the European Common Market lacked the credibility that stems from having the attributes of an optimal currency zone. The EEC was devoid of these classical features of labour market mobility, fiscal transfer mechanisms and the synchronisation of national business cycles that characterise an optimal currency zone. Furthermore, economic divergences between the core and peripheral regions continued to generate centrifugal forces that threatened the internal cohesion of the EEC. Although the EEC failed to conform to the conditions necessary to establish an optimal currency area, the problem of asymmetrical shocks and the question of which countries would incur the main burden of adjustment in the event of monetary union, were to inform earlier experiments towards EMU. Indeed, these problems were already acknowledged and highlighted in Mundell's original theory of optimal currency areas. This chapter will examine the first experiment known as the "snake in the tunnel" and some of the theoretical problems associated with a system of fixed exchange rates.

The theory of Optimum Currency Areas

In order to shed some theoretical insights into the problems, which inform the political debates over the efficacy of monetary union, it might be useful to briefly examine the theory of Optimum Currency Areas. The seminal theory of OCAs has been attributed to the analysis formulated by R.A. Mundell (1961). The theory is based on a simple two-country/region model. It is assumed that countries A and B possess separate national currencies that operate under a fixed exchange rate regime and that both are in a state of balance of payments equilibrium and full employment. If a shift in demand occurs from country B to country A, then B will experience unemployment and A will, *ceteris paribus*, experience an increase in inflation. Insofar as prices are allowed to rise in A, the shift in the terms of trade will enable B to adjust through exchange rate devaluations and by doing so, avoid incurring the main burden of adjustment in terms of employment and output. However, if country A pursues an anti-inflationary policy, the whole burden of adjustment will be borne by country B, which will tend to experience a higher level of unemployment and a fall in output.

DOI: 10.1057/9781137371904

> The policy of surplus countries in restraining prices therefore imparts a recessive tendency to the world economy on fixed exchange rates or (more generally) to a currency area with many separate currencies ... In a currency area comprising different countries with national currencies the pace of employment in deficit countries is set by the willingness of surplus countries to inflate. But in a currency area comprising many regions and a single currency, the pace of inflation is set by the willingness of central authorities to allow unemployment in deficit areas. (Mundell, 1961, pp.656–57)

Mundell's argument in this regard was quite pertinent to the role performed by Germany under a fixed exchange rate regime in Europe (Dyson, 2008b, p.111). Since Germany was the principal surplus country, the willingness of the German monetary authorities to reflate and provide an increase in aggregate demand for the Community as a whole was quite critical. In the event of a supply shock or a recession, the behaviour of the Bundesbank was pivotal in terms of which countries incurred the greatest burden of structural adjustment. Under the former Bretton Woods system, the problem of structural adjustment was supervised by the IMF, which would intervene in its role as lender of last resort to ensure that inflationary deficit countries pursued internal adjustment by adopting an anti-inflationary policy stance rather than resorting to an external adjustment through an exchange rate devaluation. As a fixed but flexible exchange rate system characterised by a crawling peg, the Bretton Woods system was inherently asymmetrical although this was offset by the willingness of the US monetary authorities to pursue expansionary policies and perform the role of reserve currency nation by providing the necessary liquidity (Tsoukalis, 1985).

Keynes's ill-fated international clearing union or "bancor" regime proposed during the Bretton Woods negotiations in 1944 provides compelling insights into the dilemmas encountered by the European architects of a fixed exchange rate regime. The Keynes plan involved the creation of an International Clearing Union (ICU), which would act as an international central bank and issue its own currency, the bancor, the value of which would be determined at a fixed price to gold. Each member country would establish a fixed but adjustable exchange rate in relation to the bancor. International payments balances were to be settled by using the bancor as a unit of account. The bancor would have very limited convertibility; countries could purchase bancors but could not convert them into gold. In other words, bancor reserves would remain within the system to avoid the possibility of a drain on reserves. Each

DOI: 10.1057/9781137371904

country would also be allocated a quota of bancors based upon their levels of imports and exports.

The essential aim of Keynes's ICU was to prevent the onset of competitive devaluations and to mitigate the deflationary tendencies caused by the reluctance of surplus countries to reflate and stimulate aggregate demand for the deficit countries. The pre-war system governed by the gold standard had imparted a deflationary bias, which forced the deficit countries to adjust internally by imposing policies of austerity (Skidelsky, 2000, p.231). Keynes had envisaged an international system that would reverse this deflationary bias and impart an expansionary impetus, which would allow deficit countries to pursue full employment policies. This necessarily implied that the surplus countries would be obliged to incur more of the burden of adjustment. The dilemma arose that the surplus countries could continue to accumulate foreign exchange reserves almost without limit, as long as the central bank could sterilise the inflationary effects. The deficit countries, on the other hand, would eventually run out of foreign exchange reserves and be exposed to speculative attacks on their currencies. In this sense, the burden of adjustment would be borne almost entirely by the deficit countries, which would be forced to enact contractionary policies and experience higher levels of unemployment. These asymmetrical shocks would ultimately depress international effective demand and have an adverse effect on the exports of the surplus countries themselves. As Crotty contends:

> There can be no doubt that the international financial system that Keynes proposed and defended in the early 1940s had as a major objective the facilitation of high rates of growth and low rates of unemployment in its constituent countries. Under the prevailing system, serious payments imbalances created deflationary pressures on deficit countries. The ensuing contractions that developed in these countries could then spread to surplus countries through the erosion of their export markets. In the extreme instance, this chain of events had the power to generate a world-wide slump. (1983, p.62)

It was precisely the problem of structural adjustment that had informed debates between "monetarists" and "economists". In other words, if an OCA was established, which countries or regions would experience the greatest burden of structural adjustment? The "economist" strategy implied that the burden of adjustment would be imposed almost entirely on the deficit countries. Germany would emerge as the de facto nominal exchange rate anchor by virtue of the fact that the Deutsche Mark (DM) would tend to appreciate and provide a strong currency option for the system as a whole. The deficit countries, on the other hand, would be compelled to adopt more stringent anti-inflationary policies in order to align themselves to the lower German rate of inflation. The convergence of economic policies would therefore tend to conform to German ideological preferences and impart a deflationary bias within the OCA. By contrast, the "monetarist" strategy implied a more symmetrical arrangement in which the burden of adjustment between the deficit and surplus countries would be shared with the immediate pooling of reserves. This plan, however, was devoid of a mechanism or set of rules that would have prevented the transmission of inflation from the deficit to the surplus countries. In the absence of an IMF-style regulatory framework, the only resolution to the problem of structural adjustment would continue to depend on the willingness of the surplus countries or regions to either reflate or recycle their surpluses in the deficit countries/regions.

An OCA, however, is quite different from complete economic and monetary union. Whereas an OCA comprises a group of countries that share a fixed exchange rate, an economic and monetary union implied the convergence and progressive centralisation of macroeconomic policies. It also implies a certain degree of fiscal federalism in order to redistribute resources to the less developed regions. In the absence of these redistributive policies, monetary union would tend to sharpen these regional inequalities. According to Mundell, factor mobility provides the rationalising logic in the formation of an OCA. Labour mobility is identified as the ultimate solution to the problem of structural adjustment. If labour migrates from the deficit to the surplus regions, the burden of exchange rate adjustment could be eased, if not eliminated altogether. Mundell also assumes that the liberalisation of capital markets would attract capital away from the high wage regions to the low wage regions.

Mundell's neoclassical assumptions can be criticised on the grounds that the degree of labour mobility in Europe has been relatively rigid across national frontiers. The only notable exception has been the wave of post-war migration of workers from the Italian *mezzogiorno* to the northern industrial core regions in France and Germany. In fact most of the recent migration has originated from the extra-Community regions in the Middle East, northern Africa and Turkey. As long as linguistic impediments continue to exist, labour will continue to remain relatively immobile. The evidence suggests that monetary union could be undermined if economic growth and development is not promoted in the less

DOI: 10.1057/9781137371904

developed regions (Magnifico, 1971). In terms of capital mobility, the historical evidence is ambiguous but suggests that capital is more likely to be attracted and concentrated in the more developed "core" regions in which there is a virtuous circle of investment, savings and employment growth (Seers and Vaitsos, 1980).[1]

The problems confronting the issue of monetary union appeared to be quite substantial in the light of diverging national economic policies, uneven development and the necessary conditions required in promoting exchange rate convergence between the surplus and deficit countries. Although the theory of OCAs highlighted some of these issues, the eventual outcome would ultimately depend on the willingness of national governments to surrender a real or perceived sovereignty over monetary and exchange rate policies. The emergence of the dollar crisis and its global repercussions merely brought these problems into sharper focus.

The "snake in the tunnel"

Before the official abandonment of the Bretton Woods agreements in 1972–73, the Community found itself disunited and unable to formulate a common approach to the impact of exchange rate volatility and speculative flights of capital. While West Germany and Italy had allowed their currencies to float, France adopted a two-tiered regime in which all transactions on the current account were regulated but the capital account was allowed to be determined by the market (Tsoukalis, 1977, p.133). The Benelux countries, in the meantime, had adopted a joint float and had unsuccessfully proposed a joint Community float against the dollar. These discordant and disparate responses to the dollar crisis merely increased the scope for speculation. The Six were eventually able to reach a tentative accord in their negotiating stance during the Smithsonian Agreements in December 1971. The outcome of these negotiations between the Group of Ten industrial countries involved the official renunciation of gold/dollar convertibility and the unilateral devaluation of the US dollar by 9 per cent. As a result, the German mark was effectively revalued by 13.5 per cent, the Belgium franc and Dutch guilder by 11.6 per cent, the French franc by 8.6 per cent and the Italian lira by 7.5 per cent in relation to the US dollar. The Group of Ten also agreed to a modified version of fixed exchange rates which allowed managed, adjustable parities. It was agreed to increase parity bands from the

DOI: 10.1057/9781137371904

Bretton Woods margin of 1.5 per cent to 2.25 per cent in order to ease speculative propensities.

During the Paris Summit convened by the Heads of Government in February 1972, it was agreed to foster exchange rate convergence between Community member states by implementing the Smithsonian parities. It soon became evident, however, that the Smithsonian parities set at 2.25 per cent in relation to the dollar implied a margin of intra-EEC currency fluctuation of 4.5 per cent. Furthermore, under a "crawling peg" regime, the spread between two EEC currencies could reach as high as 9 per cent in the long term if one currency appreciated by the permitted 4.5 per cent while another currency depreciated by the same magnitude. Quite clearly, the magnitude of these exchange rate divergences was too high to sustain the CAP and threatened to sabotage further progress toward economic union. The Basel Agreement by the Community central banks in March reduced intra-EEC exchange rate fluctuations to 2.25 per cent, which was equivalent to the central dollar margin. It was from this agreement that the "snake in the tunnel" was born. The parameter of the "tunnel" was set at 4.5 per cent, while the "snake" was confined to a margin of 2.25 per cent. In order to keep the snake within the tunnel, European currencies would be used as a means of central bank intervention while the dollar would be deployed to prevent the snake from leaving the tunnel altogether. The six original members of the currency bloc were soon accompanied by Ireland, the UK, Denmark and Norway.

Despite the Smithsonian accords, further speculative waves engulfed international currency markets in February–March and June–July, 1972. In June a speculative attack was launched against the British pound in the wake of the worsening UK balance of payments. Large scale intervention by the Bank of England in concert with the Banque de France and the monetary authorities in Brussels failed to prevent the British withdrawal from the snake mechanism. The premature exit of the pound after only three months had exposed the institutional weakness and limited resources devoted to defend the snake regime. Encouraged by the capitulation of the European monetary authorities, speculators now targeted the Italian lira and Danish kroner.

In response to the exchange rate crisis, the Finance Ministers of the enlarged Community[2] met in Rome to discuss progress toward the second stage of the Werner Plan. At the top of their agenda were plans to increase the supervisory powers and the financial resources of the European Monetary Co-operation Fund. During the speculative attack

DOI: 10.1057/9781137371904

on the pound, the Bundesbank had refused to support central bank, open market operations because of the British insistence that debts incurred should be repaid in US dollars. In order to sterilise the inflow of US dollars in exchange for DMs, the Bundesbank was willing to allow the pound to float outside the snake mechanism (George, 1991, p.172). The ability of the EMCF to counter these speculative forces was quite limited. Endowed with a very modest fund of about 2 billion dollars which was composed of 70 per cent national currencies, 10 per cent gold and 20 per cent US dollars, the EMCF was limited to providing short-term credit to central banks under the auspices of the Bank for International Settlement. As an agent of the BIS, its autonomy was curtailed and the fund did not have the authority to act as a regional version of the IMF, nor as an embryonic European central bank. Although a degree of consensus had emerged during the Rome meeting to increase funds for the EMCF, the issue of pooling national reserves continued to pose the greatest obstacle to further progress toward monetary union (Coffey, 1977).

In late 1972 European interest rates increased sharply in relation to prevailing rates in the US, which attracted another speculative inflow of capital. On this occasion, the Italian lira was the target of these speculative attacks. Although the Italian balance of payments was in surplus, the combination of a political crisis and rising German interest rates caused a flight of capital. Despite attempts by the Banca D'Italia to stem the outflow, the lira was forced to abandon the currency peg. At the same time, confidence in the dollar had not been restored as the US current account deficit exceeded $US10bn in early 1973. After a series of meetings between the Finance Ministers of the Group of Ten, the US dollar was devalued by 10 per cent in February 1973. The second dollar devaluation signalled the demise of the Smithsonian accords and the international post-war system of fixed exchange rates. President Nixon had effectively closed the gold window. The US economy was no longer encumbered by the problem of generating a current account surplus by which to finance its capital account deficits. The US trade and budget deficits could be financed by the issuing of bonds and securities which would be purchased by the rest of the world. In other words, US interest rates would act as the sole means of regulating international liquidity while exchange rates would be governed by market forces. American policy-makers could now pursue an unfettered strategy of "benign neglect" in order to restore their international export competitiveness through successive dollar devaluations (Parboni, 1981, pp.89–90).

DOI: 10.1057/9781137371904

The dollar crisis therefore not only generated an inflationary upsurge, which had forced European governments to impose quite severe deflationary policies, but successive dollar devaluations also threatened to erode the competitiveness of European exports. The Germans, in particular, were caught in a dilemma. On the one hand, the Bundesbank was reluctant to accumulate excessive US dollars because of the perceived inflationary consequences. On the other hand, the Bundesbank was compelled to support the exchange rate of the US dollar by purchasing US bonds. The US Federal Reserve, in the meantime, attempted to persuade their German counterparts to compensate for US balance of payments deficits through a revaluation of the DM. Given this dilemma, the German authorities sought a joint Community float against the US dollar in order to prevent the internationalisation of the mark. These German proposals had encountered opposition from France and Italy a year earlier, both of whom had favoured more stringent capital controls. With the emergence of generalised currency floats, however, this opposition soon evaporated. A joint Community float against the US dollar would benefit German exports within the EEC and foster a de facto DM-zone. Moreover, the creation of an area of monetary stability would prevent the possible onset of competitive devaluations within Europe. In March 1973, the remaining members of the "snake in the tunnel" agreed to a joint float.

The impact of the oil price shocks

The singularly most important event that overshadowed all attempts to promote monetary cohesion occurred with the sudden quadrupling of oil prices by the OPEC cartel in mid-1973. Within the Community, the oil price shocks had intensified existing tensions between the high inflation, deficit countries and the low inflation, surplus countries and ultimately led to the withdrawal of France from the snake regime in January 1974. In stark contrast, the lower dependence on oil imports contributed to a sharp improvement in the US balance of payments. Whereas the EEC had relied on more than 60 per cent of their energy requirements through the importation of oil and Japan as high as 75 per cent, the American dependence was less than 50 per cent (Tanzer, 1980, p.128). The emergence of petro-dollar recycling offered considerable benefits for the US economy. Not only were oil transactions denominated in US

DOI: 10.1057/9781137371904

dollars but a high proportion of the funds generated by OPEC surpluses were invested in US bonds and equities (Al-Chalabi, 1980, p.97). The expanding OPEC markets offered considerable scope for investment and export outlets of which the US multinational corporations were the major beneficiaries, most notably in the export of armaments to the Middle East. Since US oil corporations dominated Middle East oil output, the repatriation of oil profits contributed to the improvement of the US balance of payments. Between 1972 and 1974, these oil profits were estimated to have increased from $0.8bn to over $10bn (Petras and Rhodes, 1976, p.41). Table 2.1 illustrates the impact of the oil price shocks on the balance of payments within the EEC.

The quadrupling of oil prices in mid-1973 coincided with the onset of the most severe international recession since the Second World War. Although it did not cause the recession, the oil price shocks accentuated its severity. A net transfer of about 2 per cent of income from the OECD countries to the OPEC cartel was estimated to have occurred as a result. The most visible impact of these oil price shocks, however, was experienced in the deterioration of the balance of payments of the most oil dependent countries and the subsequent adjustments required to dampen the inflationary cost-push effects. Quite severe disinflationary policies were imposed, which led to a rise in unemployment and a fall in potential output. The oil price shocks therefore acted as a profound catalyst in revealing the conflicting economic policies and diverging trends within the Community.

In West Germany, the impact of the oil price rises was absorbed quite easily because of their accumulated trade and fiscal surpluses. This was in contrast to Italy and France where both higher inflation and fiscal

TABLE 2.1 *Estimated change in the current account of EEC countries in 1974 as a result of the increase in oil prices (including secondary effects)*

Country	$US billion	Percentage of GNP
West Germany	−5.8	−1.6
France	−5.3	−2.1
Belgium/Luxembourg	−1.2	−2.5
Netherlands	−0.9	−1.5
Denmark	−0.9	−2.8
United Kingdom	−4.7	−2.7
Italy	−4.2	−3.0
Ireland	−0.2	−3.3

Source: Kruse, 1980, p.152.

DOI: 10.1057/9781137371904

deficits made them more vulnerable. In Italy, for instance, the dependence on oil imports was as high as 70 per cent and the effects of the oil price rises were estimated to have caused a 20 per cent decline in the terms of trade or equivalent to 4.5 per cent of GDP (Llewellyn and Potter, 1982, p.522). Whereas the importance assigned to price stability was paramount in West Germany, this political consensus did not exist in Italy or France. Given these divergent economic trends, further progress toward monetary union was postponed. The Council meeting by the Finance Ministers in June 1974 had failed to reach agreement on the pooling of national reserves, the financing of multilateral aid and other issues related to the second stage of the Werner Plan.

The *coup de grace* to the EMU experiment was delivered by the French government in late 1973. The onset of a balance of payments crisis set in motion a speculative attack on the franc which forced the French authorities to withdraw from the "snake in the tunnel" and allowed the currency to float. While the French authorities continued to pursue relatively expansionary policies to stimulate growth and employment, their West German counterparts adopted a more conservative anti-inflationary strategy. These diverging economic trends could no longer be reconciled as Table 2.2 demonstrates. Given the reluctance of the French authorities to sacrifice economic growth and the unwillingness of the Bundesbank to tolerate a higher rate of inflation, France's departure from the EMU experiment was inevitable. Despite a temporary re-entry in June 1975, the franc was eventually forced to withdraw once again in March 1976. Consequently, the major "monetarist" member of EMU no longer participated while the two major "economist" countries of Germany and the Netherlands remained inside the tunnel. Consequently, the EMU experiment had devolved into an exclusive DM-zone.

TABLE 2.2 *Comparative economic indicators between France and Germany, 1972–74*

	Inflation			Economic growth		
	1972	1973	1974	1972	1973	1974
France	5.9	7.2	14	5.6	6.6	4.7
Germany	5.7	7.2	7.0	3.0	5.5	0.5

Source: OECD Economic Surveys, 1972–74.

DOI: 10.1057/9781137371904

TABLE 2.3 *Annual inflation rates in the EEC, 1971–75*

	Belgium	France	Germany	Italy	N/lands	Britain
1971	4.3	5.5	5.3	4.8	7.5	9.4
1972	5.4	5.8	5.5	5.7	7.8	7.1
1973	7.0	7.3	6.9	10.4	8.0	8.1
1974	12.6	13.6	6.9	19.4	9.5	16.0
1975	12.7	11.6	5.9	17.1	10.2	24.1
Total	49.5	52.2	34.7	71.3	51.2	82.5

Source: OECD Economic Surveys, 1971–75.

Conceived in an environment of extreme exchange rate volatility after the collapse of the Bretton Woods system, the "snake in the tunnel" had provided a degree of exchange rate convergence but lacked both the financial resources and the political cohesion to defend intra-Community exchange rate parities. Diverging economic trends eventually destroyed the process of monetary integration as conflicting national imperatives superseded a common strategy. After the French withdrawal, only five of the original nine members remained in the snake mechanism. The snake found itself both mutilated and deprived of a tunnel. With the onset of the international recession and the oil price shocks, these divergent national trends could no longer be reconciled with the logic of monetary union. This was most evident in the diverging rates of inflation between member states as Table 2.3 illustrates.

From this evidence alone, the lower inflation countries of West Germany, the Netherlands and Belgium remained within the snake mechanism, while the high inflation countries were forced to adopt an independent float. West Germany became the centre of gravity to which the remaining members coalesced around. The Benelux countries and Denmark gravitated toward West Germany because of their close trading relations and the attractions offered by a stable exchange rate anchor to their small, relatively open economies. A polarisation therefore emerged between the low inflation, surplus countries of West Germany and the Netherlands, on the one hand, and the high inflation, deficit countries of Italy, France and the UK, on the other. While the former were more successful in stabilising their short-term exchange rate fluctuations, the latter were trapped in a vicious circle of currency depreciations, which merely induced higher import prices and an upsurge in the rate of inflation. This widening gulf between the two groups of countries is reflected in Table 2.4.

DOI: 10.1057/9781137371904

TABLE 2.4 *Current account balances and effective exchange rates in Europe, 1973–79*

	Current account balance (annual average $ millions)	Effective exchange rates (percentage changes)
France	-1,699	-5.7
Germany	4,375	35.8
Italy	382	-39.2
UK	-2,691	-21.6
Netherlands	629	20.0
Benelux	-710	11.8
OECD Europe	-10,991	N/A

Source: Llewellyn and Potter, 1982, p.35.

Conclusion

It can be surmised that the problem of asymmetrical shocks within a fixed exchange rate regime remained unresolved. Germany consolidated its economic dominance in Europe. The success of monetary union thus hinged critically on the strategic role performed by the Bundesbank. The accumulation of structural trade surpluses by Germany and the refusal of the Bundesbank to pursue more expansionary policies tended to impart a disinflationary impulse within the Community. If the theory that informs optimum currency areas is assumed to be relevant, then the creation of a fixed exchange rate regime will merely accentuate these asymmetrical relations between the deficit and surplus countries in the absence of a German policy of reflation. In this sense, it was the dollar-DM relationship that ultimately constrained Germany's ability to pursue a more expansionary monetary policy regardless of the Bundesbank's historical aversion to inflation. The weakness of the US dollar in relation to the DM tended to sharpen these intra-Community asymmetrical relations. Conversely, a strong dollar promoted a more symmetrical configuration within Europe. In the final analysis, however, monetary union was essentially governed by political imperatives; its ultimate fate rested on the willingness of member states to surrender their perceived monetary sovereignty to a supranational central bank. Under these circumstances, the architecture of the central bank and its willingness to act as a lender of last resort in the event of country-specific asymmetrical shocks would become absolutely critical in the survival of EMU.

DOI: 10.1057/9781137371904

Notes

1 A more detailed treatment of this regional dimension is developed in Chapter 5.

2 The UK, Ireland and Denmark signed their respective accession treaties and officially joined the EEC in 1972.

DOI: 10.1057/9781137371904

3

The European Monetary System, 1979–87

Abstract: *With the demise of the first experiment in monetary union, many critics had proclaimed that the whole enterprise was ill-conceived and doomed to failure. Another attempt to revive the project was considered highly unlikely as long as the Bundesbank remained trenchantly opposed and diverging macroeconomic trends and policies continued to characterise the internal dynamics of the European Community (EC). Rumours of its demise, however, were greatly exaggerated. The renewed dollar crisis of 1978 provided a catalyst to launch a second experiment in March 1979. The American policy of "benign neglect" had allowed the dollar to slide which, in turn, generated a renewed phase of international volatility in financial and currency markets. The obvious threat to intra-Community exchange rate stability posed by this renewed speculative volatility convinced the newly elected Social Democratic government of Chancellor Schmidt that a new exchange rate regime was required within the Community. This became even more urgent after the failure of German-US measures to stabilise the dollar. With the recent election of President d'Estaing of France, Schmidt had found an accommodating ally in reviving the EMU project.*

Lucarelli, Bill. *Endgame for the Euro: A Critical History.* Basingtoke: Palgrave Macmillan, 2013.
DOI: 10.1057/9781137371904.

Introduction

With the demise of the first experiment in monetary union, many critics had proclaimed that the whole enterprise was ill-conceived and doomed to failure. Another attempt to revive the project was considered highly unlikely as long as the Bundesbank remained trenchantly opposed and diverging macroeconomic trends and policies continued to characterise the internal dynamics of the European Community. Rumours of its demise, however, were greatly exaggerated. The renewed dollar crisis of 1978 provided a catalyst to launch a second experiment in March 1979. The American policy of "benign neglect" had allowed the dollar to slide which, in turn, generated a renewed phase of international volatility in financial and currency markets. In the course of 1977, the German mark had appreciated by about 10 per cent in relation to the US dollar. At the same time, however, the French franc had depreciated by 6 per cent and the Italian lira by a dramatic 15 per cent against the German mark. The obvious threat to intra-Community exchange rate stability posed by these re-alignments convinced the newly elected Social Democratic government of Chancellor Schmidt that a new exchange rate regime was required within the Community. This became even more urgent after the failure of German-US measures to stabilise the dollar. With the recent election of President d'Estaing of France, Schmidt had found an accommodating ally in reviving the EMU project.

The political rationale

The earliest proposals for the re-launching of the EMU project came from Roy Jenkins – a former President of the Commission – in October 1977 (Jenkins, 1978). These proposals formed the basis of the Schmidt initiative and the accord reached with d'Estaing in April 1978 at the European Council meeting in Copenhagen. Three months later, at the European Council meeting in Bremen, the Franco-German proposals were endorsed and the Ministers of Finance were instructed to formulate the institutional and technical details. The legal and institutional structure of the European Monetary System (EMS) was finally adopted by the European Council in Brussels on 5 and 6 December 1978. According to this agreement, the EMS was expected to enter into its formal operational phase within two years of its official launch in March 1979. The

DOI: 10.1057/9781137371904

Greek and British representatives chose to postpone their membership of the EMS.

In short, the EMS was, like its predecessor, essentially a Franco-German initiative. A similar logic governed the new accord: while the French sought German support for their exchange rate, which had come under renewed speculative attack, Germany demanded support for closer co-ordination of national economic policies. In other words, the trade-off involved the French aims of stabilising the CAP and the German desire to prevent the onset of competitive devaluations which would ultimately threaten their industrial exports. However, Schmidt's EMU proposals were staunchly opposed by the Bundesbank, which feared that their independence would be imperilled and inflationary pressures would be rekindled. In order to placate the Bundesbank, Schmidt's plan involved an anti-inflationary bias and strict limits imposed on the use of US dollars in foreign exchange rate interventions. In its rudimentary form, the Schmidt plan had envisaged the following features:

- Exchange rate interventions to be made in Community currencies with stringent limits imposed on the use of US dollars.
- Monthly settlement of payments with the debtor incurring the exchange rate risk.
- The introduction of a very short-term credit facility to provide automatic financial aid to member states experiencing an exchange rate crisis. The fund would be limited to a system of national quotas and all settlements would be made within three months through a European unit of account.
- In order to impose a greater degree of rigour to the process of exchange rate convergence, inflation targets would be set.

The Italian monetary authorities were initially ambivalent about the revival of monetary union. They had been pursuing a strategy which had borne considerable success in promoting the expansion of their exports. This strategy involved an appreciation of the lira against the US dollar, on the one hand, and a depreciation of the lira against the German mark, on the other. Consequently, Italian exports gradually shifted away from the US market and increased their share of the European market at the expense of France and Germany. Italy's decision to join the EMS was thus primarily motivated by political considerations but conditional on a wider margin of fluctuation of 6 per cent for the lira in the Exchange Rate Mechanism (ERM).

TABLE 3.1 *Economic indicators, 1978–82*

Countries	1978	1979	1980	1981	1982
Countries with low inflation					
Belgium/Luxembourg (a)	−1.0	−2.8	−4.2	−4.1	−3.1
(b)	4.5	4.5	6.6	7.6	8.7
(c)	107.7	104.9	100.8	97.8	88.0
The Netherlands (a)	−1.1	−1.3	−1.8	2.0	2.7
(b)	4.1	4.2	6.5	6.7	5.9
(c)	123.5	120.5	117.9	115.9	120.1
West Germany (a)	1.4	−0.8	−1.9	−0.9	0.5
(b)	2.7	4.1	5.5	5.9	5.3
(c)	109.3	107.8	102.0	98.4	100.4
Countries with high inflation					
France (a)	1.5	0.9	−0.6	−0.8	−2.9
(b)	9.3	10.6	13.5	13.3	12.0
(c)	94.0	96.1	99.3	101.1	97.0
Italy (a)	2.4	1.7	−2.5	−2.3	−1.6
(b)	12.2	14.7	23.0	17.7	16.6
(c)	76.1	78.7	85.9	89.6	92.3

(a) Current account balances (percentage of GDP); (b) Inflation rates (average annual percentage increase); (c) Real exchange rates (1970=100)

Source: OECD Main Economic Indicators, 1983.

From the standpoint of the British authorities, the Franco-German agreement had aroused deep suspicions. They had, doubtless, not easily forgotten their disastrous experience in the "snake" experiment, which had witnessed an unprecedented attack on the pound sterling and was responsible for an estimated 30 per cent loss of their foreign exchange reserves. Moreover, with the opening of upstream operations in their North Sea oil venture, the pound had become an oil currency and tended to appreciate against the EMS currencies. Given these circumstances, the UK authorities postponed their participation in the EMS, although the pound sterling would constitute one of the currencies in the European Currency Unit (ECU) basket. Although the political rationale in re-launching the EMU project was paramount, the underlying economic conditions were also favourable. Between 1978 and 1982 there appeared overwhelming evidence of a convergence of critical economic indicators after the tensions generated by the oil price shocks. This evidence is highlighted in Table 3.1.

DOI: 10.1057/9781137371904

The intervention and financing mechanisms

Although it is possible to identify a certain degree of continuity between the EMS and its "snake" predecessor, important differences were evident in relation to the role performed by the European Currency Unit and the mechanism of the "divergence indicator." Furthermore, the EMS was endowed with more than twice the financial resources than the previous contributions to the EMCF to defend agreed parities and was characterised by a greater degree of exchange rate flexibility. These institutional features were accompanied by a more coherent and robust set of regional and structural funds; more than 200 billion ECUs were allocated to these funds in the first five years (Coffey, 1987, p.23). At the very core of the EMS was the Exchange Rate Mechanism in which participating countries were obliged to keep their bilateral exchange rates within the agreed margins of fluctuation. Although these central rates were expressed in terms of the ECU, the compulsory intervention rates were defined on a bilateral basis. The Brussels resolution states that "in principle, interventions will be made in participating currencies" (Article 3.3) and that "intervention in participating currencies is compulsory when the intervention points defined by the fluctuation margins are reached" (Article 3.4). A central system of bilateral parities was thus established in which intra-ERM margins of fluctuation were limited to within 2.25 per cent either side of parity, with the exception of Italy and Ireland in which the margin was set at (+/–) 6 per cent. Beyond these bilateral limits, compulsory intervention was enforced by the Brussels resolution.

The EMS Agreement was the outcome of a series of political compromises between potential debtors and creditors. The former were guaranteed lines of credit to defend the agreed parities in order to promote a smooth exchange rate adjustment. The overriding objective of potential creditors, on the other hand, was focused on the domestic monetary consequences of the intervention and financing operations. Their concern was to avoid excessive liquidity and credit creation by imposing specific commitments on the debtor countries to introduce the necessary economic policy adjustments. These provisions were enshrined in the strict limits in the period of repayment under the Very Short-Term Financing facility (VSTF) and by the IMF-type conditionality rules for medium term credit. The use of ECUs was initially confined to 50 per cent of settlements, while members of the VSTF were obliged to deposit 20 per cent of their gold and dollar reserves against the issuing of ECUs.

DOI: 10.1057/9781137371904

Consequently, both the limited use of ECUs in official transactions and their non-convertibility had failed to prevent the Community's continued dependence on the US dollar. Indeed, over two thirds of all official interventions between 1979 and 1985 were denominated in the US dollar. Since the ECU was devoid of legal tender status, its function was confined as a unit of account replacing the former European Unit of Account (EUA).

The EMS was therefore characterised by two major innovations: the Exchange Rate Mechanism and the European Currency Unit. The ERM could be described as an "adjustable peg" regime by which marginal interventions were compulsory. Intra-marginal interventions were also possible and became the most frequent type of market intervention by central banks. These often involved swap agreements between central banks before the compulsory margins were reached. For instance, if the Italian lira depreciated to the lower limits of its permitted band in relation to the German mark, the Bank of Italy was obliged to intervene by selling marks and purchasing lira. Should the lira overshoot the divergence threshold, marginal intervention was compulsory and the VSTF was deployed to provide lines of credit between the central banks in order to avoid destabilising speculation against the lira. Originally it was agreed that the debt should be settled within 45 days after the end of each month but with the signing of the Basle-Nyborg Agreement of 1987, the period of settlement was extended to 75 days.

The other major feature of the EMS was the creation of ECUs which were devised on the basis of a basket of currencies calculated as a proportion of each member's GDP, trade and short-term credit quotas. Each currency had a central rate expressed in ECUs. These central rates could be changed by a voluntary agreement between the central banks and the EC Commission. By linking together the ECU-related central rates, a parity grid could be devised by a series of bilateral rates. In other words, each currency was calculated as a central rate of the ECU rather than in terms of the ECU. As a result, depreciating currencies experienced a fall in their relative weight in the ECU basket while appreciating currencies would increase their relative weight. In the long run, there developed a natural tendency for strong currencies to gradually increase their relative value in terms of the ECU, which eventually entrenched the asymmetrical dynamics of the system.[1]

The most innovative feature of the ECU was the introduction of a "divergence indicator," (expressed as a percentage), which measured the

DOI: 10.1057/9781137371904

extent to which a given currency was approaching its maximum divergence threshold. If it reached 75 per cent, the currency had approached its divergence threshold and the monetary authorities were obliged but not compelled to intervene (Appendix 3A). Since the weight of a particular currency influenced the market rate of the ECU expressed in that currency, the market rate could only deviate from its central rate by a percentage necessarily less than the maximum 2.25 per cent or 6 per cent. As a result, the maximum divergence was higher the smaller the weight of the currency and, conversely, lower the greater the weight of the currency in the ECU basket. Table 3.2 demonstrates these differing maximum spreads and divergence thresholds.

In order to issue ECUs, central banks deposited 20 per cent of their gold and dollar reserves with the EMCF. These official ECUs were intended to serve as a reserve asset, though subject to various restrictions. As a non-convertible instrument of credit, ECUs could be used as the official numeraire in intra-ERM settlements. It was envisaged by the EMS agreements that the ECU would promote a more equitable sharing of the risks between creditors and debtors. However, given the "strong currency" option adopted by the weaker members, the EMS evolved into an asymmetrical regime dominated by the deutschmark. Indeed, the growth of private ECUs, not anticipated by the EMS Agreement, stemmed largely as a substitute for the DM because of the reluctance of the Bundesbank to internationalise the German currency. In an international environment characterised by exchange rate volatility and rising nominal interest rates, the low risk premium of the ECU basket and its lower interest rates for borrowers, increased the demand for private ECUs throughout the 1980s.

TABLE 3.2 *Maximum divergence spreads and divergence thresholds (average rates from September 1984 to February 1985)*

(1) Currency	(2)Maximum spread (%)	Divergence threshold (%) (75% of (2), (+/−))
BRF/LFR	2.06	1.545
DM	1.53	1.148
HFL	2.02	1.515
DKR	2.19	1.643
FF	1.82	1.365
LIT	5.4	4.05
IRL	2.22	1.665

Source: Commission Departments.

DOI: 10.1057/9781137371904

The international dimension

Although the EMS provided a considerable degree of exchange rate cohesion, it failed to promote monetary sovereignty in relation to the US dollar. Just like its snake predecessor, the survival of the EMS was critically dependent upon the DM-dollar relationship. The EMS was thus still vulnerable to exogenous shocks emanating from the volatility of the US dollar. From this standpoint, the relative success of the EMS during the first half of the 1980s was determined, to a large extent, on the sharp appreciation of the US dollar. The objective conditions were favourable in terms of the cyclical recovery in 1982–87, which was accompanied by a fall in oil prices. Intra-ERM exchange rate cohesion and the convergence of economic policies could be fostered in this favourable international environment.

In stark contrast, the US dollar had been subjected to chronic instability in 1977–78. The prospect of a prolonged deficit in the US current account and the inability of the government to dampen inflationary forces had provoked a renewed dollar sell-off by international investors. At the same time, the sharp appreciation of the mark generated tensions within the Community. In response to the slide in the US dollar, the Carter administration was persuaded to abandon their policy of "benign neglect" and actively pursued a more interventionist strategy. US policy makers propounded the "locomotive theory" in which they attempted to persuade the major surplus countries of Japan and Germany to pump prime their economies, arguing that a concerted fiscal stimulus would redress the widening trade and payments imbalances and generate a sustained recovery. Both the German and Japanese authorities, however, were quite reluctant to pursue a more expansionary programme because of the inflationary risks involved. In 1977 and 1978, the US economy experienced a current account deficit of $15.2bn and $13.2bn respectively. At the same time, official claims on the US Treasury increased by around $35bn and $32bn respectively. In other words, the US Treasury was forced to replenish its reserves by borrowings in foreign capital markets. Table 3.3 illustrates these growing trade imbalances between the three major capitalist economies.

The failure of German-US negotiations to manage the dollar slide posed a serious dilemma for the German monetary authorities. They could either curtail the demand for DM-denominated assets by purchasing US bonds and securities thereby financing the US current account deficit, or

DOI: 10.1057/9781137371904

TABLE 3.3 *(1) Balance of trade and (2) Current account for the US, Germany and Japan, 1977–80 ($US billions)*

	1977	1978	1979	1980
USA (1)	−30.9	−33.8	−29.5	−25.0
(2)	−15.2	−13.5	−0.3	0.1
Germany (1)	19.3	15.5	17.7	10.0
(2)	4.3	8.9	−5.8	−15.5
Japan (1)	17.3	24.6	1.8	0
(2)	10.9	16.5	−8.6	−10.8

Source: OECD Main Economic Indicators, 1982.

they could re-launch the EMU project as a means by which the reserve currency status of the DM would be confined within the Community. The former option would have required excessive intervention by the Bundesbank in close concert with their American counterparts. Given the fact that unsterilised, open market operations were anathema to the Bundesbank because of the excessive creation of liquidity and the inflationary risks involved, agreement over a target zone for the dollar/DM exchange rate was untenable from the standpoint of the German monetary authorities. The second option offered greater strategic advantages. EMU would absorb and deflect demand for DM-denominated assets by making other European currencies closer substitutes for the DM.

Carter's neo-Keynesianism was soon replaced by a more orthodox monetarist strategy with the Presidential victory of Reagan in 1980 and the appointment of Paul Volcker as the incumbent Governor of the Federal Reserve Board. With the onset of the second oil price shocks in 1979, the OECD countries were compelled to enact restrictive fiscal and monetary policies, which had the effect of dampening the level of effective demand and contributed to the international recession of 1979–82. Germany was especially affected by the oil price rises as the trade balance went into the red in 1979–81. Given these unusual circumstances, the first two years of the EMS were characterised by the relative weakness of the German mark. At the same time, a strong dollar policy was adopted by the Reagan administration. The dollar rose sharply between July 1980 and February 1981, estimated at about 20 per cent on a trade weighted average. US nominal interest rates also rose sharply, attracting a considerable inflow of capital.

DOI: 10.1057/9781137371904

Quite contrary to expectations, the German mark did not perform the strong currency option in the first two years of the EMS transitional period. The relative weakness of the mark, however, militated against the inherent asymmetrical tendencies of the system and contributed to the stability and cohesion of intra-ERM exchange rates. These empirical observations lend credence to the contention that the dollar/DM relationship was absolutely critical in the behaviour of the ERM. In other words, if the German mark appreciated against the dollar it was likely to appreciate against the other ERM currencies. Conversely, a relative, nominal depreciation of the mark against the US dollar tended to promote a more symmetrical configuration within the ERM. The most plausible explanation for this inverse relationship is the fact that the mark was viewed by international investors and other financial agents as a close substitute for the US dollar. An exchange rate depreciation of the dollar therefore induced a flight of capital into either mark or yen denominated assets (Padoa-Schioppa, 1984, p.130).

As the EMS jointly floated downwards against the dollar between 1980 and 1985, the American domestic market provided an expanding outlet for European exports which, in turn, imparted a powerful stimulus for the cyclical recovery after 1982. German trade surpluses re-appeared. As the recovery gained momentum, however, the disparities between the surplus poles of Germany and the Netherlands, on the one hand, and the deficit poles of Italy and France, on the other hand, generated an undercurrent of potential conflict. These underlying tensions were temporarily contained by the fall in oil prices and the rapid expansion of the US economy, which provided an engine of growth for the OECD countries as a whole. In retrospect, the contradictory US strategy of tight monetary policies accompanied by expansionary fiscal policies, which were partly driven by increased military spending, could not be sustained as long as the US continued to accumulate persistent current account deficits. The relative strength of the dollar was not induced by a substantial improvement in the American trade deficit, or by a recovery of its industrial export competitiveness. Instead, the massive inflow of capital was governed almost entirely by the inducement of high nominal interest rates. Figure 3.1 illustrates short-term interest rate trends between 1975 and 1985 in the United States.

By increasing nominal interest rates and attracting short-term capital, the American economy was absorbing world savings, which had a negative impact on world investment, most notably in Europe. This was offset, in the short-term, by an increase in European exports to the

DOI: 10.1057/9781137371904

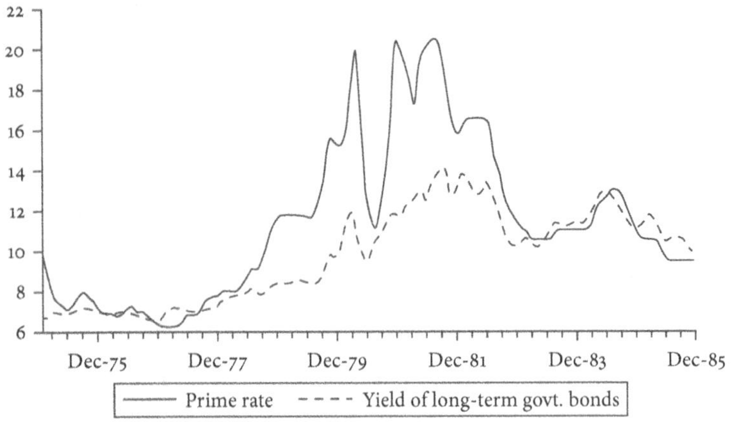

FIGURE 3.1 *United States interest rates, 1975–85 (%, pa)*

American market through a real exchange rate depreciation. In short, a virtuous circle had been set in motion in which the US economy provided an outlet for European and East Asian exports, while the savings of the latter were recycled to finance the burgeoning US current account deficits. This virtuous circle, however, was only possible as long as the dollar continued to appreciate and protectionist impulses were contained in the United States. The strong dollar policy in the first term of the Reagan administration generated two contradictory outcomes. Although the strong dollar and high nominal interest rates contributed to a curtailment of domestic inflation, it also imparted a negative impact on US export competitiveness, which was reflected in the deterioration of the balance of payments. The US trade deficit had increased from an average of $US27bn in 1978–80 to $US148bn in 1985, while the current account deficit deteriorated from $US4bn to about $US128bn over the same period (Parboni, 1986). By March 1985, the dollar was estimated to have appreciated by more than 30 per cent on a trade weighted average since the beginning of 1981. International pressure began to mount for a sustained dollar devaluation, especially after the realisation that the US economy had become a net debtor for the first time since the turn of the century. This was accompanied by a growing protectionist sentiment in the US Congress. The Reagan administration could either succumb to these protectionist demands or divert them through a dollar devaluation. In light of these events, a more interventionist policy emerged in contrast to the prevailing neoliberal paradigm that had informed US exchange rate policies.

During the second term, the Reagan administration pursued a strategy not too dissimilar to that of the Carter years by attempting to persuade Germany and Japan to adopt more expansionary policies. Predictably enough, the German and Japanese governments were reluctant to accommodate these demands. With the breakdown of macroeconomic policy co-ordination between the major industrial countries (the G-7), the central bankers of these countries launched a series of concerted interventions in order to avert a crash landing of the US dollar. An estimated $US12bn was mobilised in March 1985 to engineer a soft landing. Within a year, the dollar had depreciated by 35 per cent on a trade weighted average; the dollar/mark rate had fallen from 3.47 to 2.25 and its yen value from 260 to 175. Figure 3.2 compares the real effective exchange rates of Germany and the United States between 1973 and 1997.

After the Plaza Accords of September 1985, another concerted central bank intervention was orchestrated to counter the mounting speculation in global currency markets. The failure of Germany and Japan to stimulate their economies as the US has requested during the Plaza Summit only provoked US officials to "talk down" the dollar in what soon developed into a dangerous game of monetary brinkmanship (Funabashi, 1988). Although this American strategy eventually persuaded the Japanese to pursue a more expansionary policy after the stock market crash of October 1987, the German authorities remained intransigent. Quite simply, German exports were not as dependent on the US domestic market

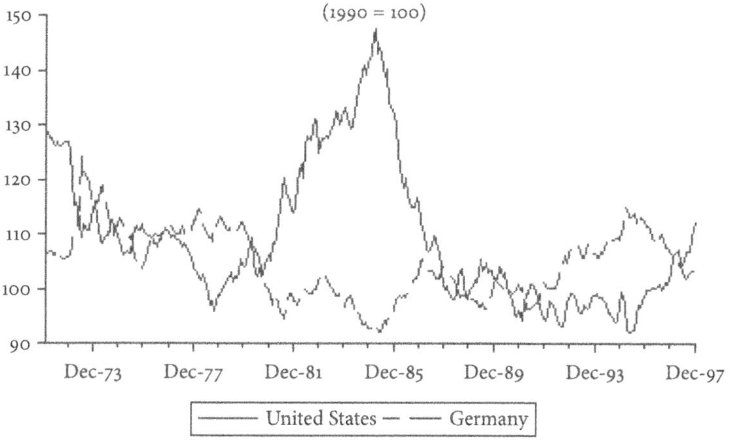

FIGURE 3.2 *Real effective exchange rates: United States and Germany, 1973–97*

DOI: 10.1057/9781137371904

as those of Japan. Whereas only about 10 per cent of German exports were destined for the American market, the EEC had accounted for about a third of total German exports.

Consequently, the maintenance of a stable exchange rate regime in Europe, embodied by the EMS, represented the primary German concern and had informed their negotiating stance during the Plaza and Louvre summit meetings. As the dollar rapidly fell from 1985 onwards, a vicious circle developed with the onset of inter-state rivalries over markets and investment outlets (Parboni, 1986). It was in this volatile environment that international summits were convened to engineer a "soft landing" of the US dollar and to co-ordinate macroeconomic policies. The ultimate failure of these summits to resolve the basic core of the problem – US deficits and dollar instability – hastened widespread financial panic in world financial markets, which culminated in the stock market crashes of 1987 and 1989. The sharp decline of the US dollar had intensified tensions within the EMS. Although the first major re-alignment in April 1986 was managed quite smoothly, the second major re-alignment in January 1987 caused a minor eruption as the French franc fell below the divergence threshold. The EMS central banks mobilised over $US10bn in open market operations to maintain parities. The weakness of the dollar therefore rebounded within the EMS. Yet despite these external shocks, the EMS experiment had survived. Its internal cohesion had withstood one of the most turbulent episodes in post-war financial history. The extent to which this cohesion and stability could be preserved, however, hinged on the strategic role performed by Germany.

Conclusion

Conceived as a Franco-German accord between President d'Estaing and Chancellor Schmidt, the EMS signalled a high point in the construction of the European monetary edifice and became the blueprint for the modern evolution of the euro. Despite initial resistance from the Bundesbank, the internal financial mechanisms of the EMS provided a more coherent and flexible means of exchange rate adjustment than its "snake" predecessor. Despite these innovations, the first decade of the EMS experiment suggests that its relative success was largely due to a favourable international environment. Most of the period from 1978 to 1985 was characterised by a strong dollar, falling oil prices and a sustained

DOI: 10.1057/9781137371904

international recovery from the recession of 1979–81. The US domestic market acted as the engine of growth for the European recovery. A virtuous circle was set in motion in which European exports increased their penetration of the American market, while the US attracted a net inflow of investment from Europe and Japan. The reversal of these propitious, external factors with the onset of the severe recession of the early 1990s, however, provoked a series of exchange rate crises.

Appendix 3A: The Divergence Indicator

The "divergence indicator" is calculated in two stages:

(1) By calculating the premium (P) or discount (D) shown by the market rate of the ECU in terms of that currency against its ECU-related central rate.
(2) By comparing the result obtained with the maximum divergence spread (MDS). The MDS for each currency is assigned an index of 100. A currency therefore reaches its divergence threshold when the index is 75.

Expressed as a formula, the indicator is calculated as follows:

P or D = ECU market rate – ECU central rate
(Divided by) ________
ECU central rate

The following example illustrates this equation:
The rate of the Belgium franc on 17 June 1982 = 45.2961 (ECU)
The ECU-related central rate of the Belgium franc = 44.9704
The maximum divergence spread of the Belgium franc = 2.9704
Therefore:

$$P = \frac{45.2961 - 44.9704}{44.9704} \times 100 = 72\%$$

$$DI = \frac{0.72}{2.0668} \times 100 = 35$$

Note

1 In the Maastricht Treaty of 1992 it was agreed to freeze these bilateral rates.

4
The German Ascendancy

Abstract: *In the study of international political economy, the concept of "hegemony" has acquired a strategic meaning. Whether implicitly or explicitly, the term applies to one country or a group of nation-states, which form a dominant power bloc within a definite hierarchy of nation-states. In the "world system" literature this configuration is viewed as a zero-sum game between the dominant core, satellite and peripheral states (Wallerstein, 1979 & 2003). With the end of the Cold War, a multi-polar system of Japan, the European Community and the United States emerged as the dominant, core group of states. The recent ascendancy of China could also reinforce this multi-polarity of the world system. With the demise of the post-war system of Pax Americana this hegemonic transition might witness the emergence of trading blocs and exclusive currency zones gravitating around these hegemonic core regions.*

Lucarelli, Bill. *Endgame for the Euro: A Critical History.* Basingtoke: Palgrave Macmillan, 2013.
DOI: 10.1057/9781137371904.

 DOI: 10.1057/9781137371904

Introduction

> Undoubtedly the fact of hegemony presupposes that account be taken of the interests and the tendencies of the groups over which hegemony is to be exercised and that a certain compromise equilibrium should be formed – in other words, that the leading group should make sacrifices of an economic-corporate kind. But there is no doubt that such sacrifices and such a compromise cannot touch the essential; for though hegemony is ethical-political, it must be economic, must necessarily be based on the decisive function exercised by the leading group in the decisive nucleus of economic activity. (Gramsci, 1971, p.161)

In the study of international political economy, the concept of "hegemony" has acquired a strategic meaning. Whether implicitly or explicitly, the term applies to one country or a group of nation-states, which form a dominant power bloc within a definite hierarchy of nation-states. In the "world system" literature this configuration is viewed as a zero-sum game between the dominant core, satellite and peripheral states (Wallerstein, 1979 & 2003). With the end of the Cold War, a multi-polar system of Japan, the European Community and the United States emerged as the dominant, core group of states. The recent ascendancy of China could also reinforce this multi-polarity of the world system. With the demise of the post-war system of *Pax Americana* this hegemonic transition might witness the emergence of trading blocs and exclusive currency zones gravitating around these hegemonic core regions.

Within the European Community, Germany's hegemonic role was confined to the economic sphere. Since the Second World War, the EC was quite successful in mediating between the revival of German economic power and the containment of German politico-military ambitions.[1] The other crucial historical condition was the construction of a European *cordon sanitaire* to counter the perceived threat of Soviet westward expansion. In the post-Cold War era and after the re-unification of Germany, Europe could now project a more independent foreign policy and incorporate the former socialist states of eastern Europe. From the perspective of France, monetary union was viewed as a means of anchoring the newly unified German state firmly within the European sphere. The realisation of monetary union was therefore closely entwined with these strategic and political re-alignments. Even before German re-unification, however, the evolution of EMU

DOI: 10.1057/9781137371904

was governed by the imperatives of German neo-mercantilism. EMU was therefore likely to reproduce the German model based upon the creation of an independent central bank, which would emulate the policies and structure of the Bundesbank. But the rise of German neo-mercantilism could also have quite adverse implications for the peripheral, deficit countries. These asymmetrical relations within Europe, with Germany acting as the hegemonic core state, could generate powerful centrifugal forces and threaten the very survival of the European project.

Germany and the problem of asymmetry

In contrast to the Bretton Woods regime in which the American financial system performed the role of world "central banker" with the issuing of international reserves, the German financial system remained firmly anchored to the imperatives of German neo-mercantilism. Whereas the US ran successive current account deficits and presided over the export of capital, Germany experienced persistent and cumulative balance of payments surpluses and a substantial build-up of foreign exchange reserves. Even though the export of capital from Germany increased rapidly during the 1980s and 1990s, the Bundesbank was very reluctant to allow the mark to acquire an international reserve currency status.[2] Both the critical mass of the German economy and its close trading relations with other EMS countries elevated Germany's economic power to impose its economic preferences on the final blueprint for monetary union. In this sense, the EMS could be portrayed as a hierarchical regime with Germany at the very apex. The problem of asymmetry was thus closely related to Germany's strategic trade relations within the EMS.

> To mix a metaphor: Germany is at the heart of the European economy, while all the other economies are peripheral. Economically, Europe may be defined as a German zone. This zone includes all countries that send a significant share of their exports (15% or more) to Germany and at least half of their total exports to the German economic zone, including Germany itself. Germany in turn sends half of its exports to the periphery of its economic zone, but no individual country absorbs more than 5–6 per cent of its exports (except Holland and France, each of which accounts for almost 10

per cent of German exports). This configuration of trade makes economic relations asymmetrical. (Parboni, 1981, p.91)

Although the problem of asymmetrical intra-EC trade and payments relations was acknowledged during the Bremen and Brussels summits, which had launched the EMS, the gravitational pull of the German economy was irreversible. Rather than sharing the burden of adjustment, the main burden was imposed on the weaker, deficit countries. The Bundesbank preserved its staunch independence, while Germany was able to pursue relatively autonomous monetary policies within the EMS but was constrained by its relationship with the US dollar and US monetary policies. In short, the dollar/DM relationship ultimately dictated intra-ERM exchange rate alignments. The continued volatility of the dollar and the inflationary consequences of US domestic policies impelled the ERM countries to peg their currencies to the German mark. As a result, German interest rates acted as the unofficial anchor or benchmark within the EMS as Figure 4.1 demonstrates. While the German monetary authorities were able to determine their exchange rate policies through interest rate adjustments, the deficit countries of France and Italy increasingly resorted to the imposition of exchange rate and capital controls. Insofar as the EMS was characterised by a "crawling peg" regime similar to the Bretton Woods system, central banks were not compelled to enforce parities in the medium and long-term. To be sure, compulsory interventions on the margins through the automatic operation of the VSTF were not very frequent. This appears to suggest

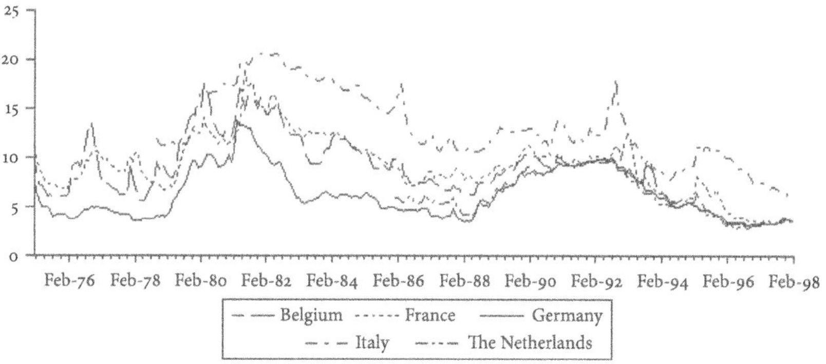

FIGURE 4.1 *Short-term interest rates in the EMS, 1975–98 (three months, % pa)*

DOI: 10.1057/9781137371904

that intra-marginal interventions were the norm, which implied that the burden of exchange rate adjustment was borne largely by the weaker, deficit members of the EMS.

These empirical observations of the internal dynamics of the EMS support the proposition that there was an inherent asymmetry with Germany acting as the de facto *Nth* country and providing an exchange rate anchor for the system as a whole. The problem of asymmetry, however, was not in itself a major obstacle to the maintenance of exchange rate stability. The real problem was with the role performed by the *Nth* country. Under the fixed but adjustable exchange rate system of Bretton Woods, the *Nth* country – the United States – provided an expansionary impetus for the system as a whole, while the US financial system was willing and structurally capable of acting as an international financial intermediary. By incurring successive current account deficits, the American financial system was acting as a financial intermediary by borrowing in the short-term in order to lend in the long-term. The US also provided liquidity for the world economy in order to prevent a drain on gold reserves. In stark contrast, the German economy imparted a deflationary tendency within the EMS and its financial sector was unwilling to act as a financial intermediary for the system as a whole. These constraints were the product of the DM/dollar relationship and the German neo-mercantilist propensity to accumulate trade surpluses.

In regard to the first constraint, a strong dollar tended to impart a higher degree of symmetry within the ERM, while a weak dollar induced a greater degree of intra-ERM exchange rate divergence. This inverse relationship was based on the close substitute between the dollar and the mark by international financial agents. The inherently "anti-Keynesian" stance of the Bundesbank enshrined the objective of price stability as the cornerstone of German macroeconomic policy. By doing so, however, a disinflationary impulse was transmitted throughout the EMS zone. While the German authorities pursued a trade off between economic growth and low inflation in order to promote monetary stability, the other deficit member countries were forced to trade off economic growth and exchange rate stability (Ferri, 1990, p.6). Given the narrow margins of exchange rate divergence imposed by the EMS agreement, the scope for exchange rate adjustment by the deficit countries was quite limited. Consequently, most of the ERM countries adopted a "strong currency" option by aligning themselves with the anti-inflationary strategy of the Bundesbank. Although this strategy fostered greater exchange

DOI: 10.1057/9781137371904

rate cohesion and discipline within the EMS, evident by the gradual convergence of national inflation rates, the ultimate cost was the legacy of relatively low rates of economic growth and high rates of cyclical unemployment. Disinflationary policies thus contributed to the onset of "Eurosclerosis" during the 1980s. By 1986, the average unemployment rate in the Community had increased from 4.7 per cent in 1975–80 to around 11 per cent. On the other hand, the rate of inflation had fallen from an average of 12 per cent to 3.7 per cent over the same period (Guerrieri and Padoan, 1989, p.2).

In terms of the second constraint, the inability of German finance capital to become the centre of payments for the EMS as a whole appears to be closely linked to the structural relationship between German finance and industry. These links, which express themselves in the form of interlocking directorships and cross-ownership, prevented the internationalisation of German finance capital. In other words, German finance capital lacked the degree of liquidity and autonomy that one associates with the London and New York capital markets. The German financial system was instead driven by the imperatives of industrial capital and the logic of maintaining German export competitiveness (Edwards and Fischer, 1994). In this sense, the EMS provided a greater degree of stability in its real effective exchange rate in relation to the US dollar, which contributed to the maintenance of Germany's export competitiveness. German exports were concentrated mostly in the capital goods and manufacturing sectors, which accounted for almost two-thirds of total exports, while one quarter of the economy was devoted to the export sector, which employed over a third of German workers. In order to counteract an appreciating exchange rate in relation to markets outside the Community, the German authorities pursued a rigorous anti-inflationary strategy which had, more or less, offset any short-term loss of export competitiveness caused by a rise in the nominal exchange rate.

Within Europe, however, the maintenance of exchange rate stability through the Exchange Rate Mechanism contributed to the promotion of German exports, which enjoyed an oligopolistic advantage and a relatively high elasticity of demand. At the same time, the accumulation of trade surpluses had the effect of increasing the share of profits in the economy as a whole. Since the increase in the profit share was not necessarily at the expense of the wages share, redistributional struggles between capital and labour were either averted or moderated (Kalecki, 1971).[3] It would be plausible to contend that this export-driven logic of the

DOI: 10.1057/9781137371904

German economy supported its "social market" policies. The accumulation of structural trade surpluses in Germany could be explained largely by the composition of its exports in finished manufactured goods, which enjoyed an oligopolistic advantage in the European market (Bulmer and Paterson, 1987). A high nominal exchange rate also encouraged the process of industrial restructuring and technological re-conversion through an increase in the capital–output ratio. In order to maintain their dominant share of these markets, intra-EC exchange rate cohesion was essential. From the standpoint of extra-EC exports from Germany, any loss of competitiveness through a nominal exchange rate appreciation was compensated by a superior anti-inflationary performance.

The EMS thus provided a relatively stable monetary zone to which most of their exports were destined, while fortifying the German economy from the destabilising impact of a volatile US dollar. At the same time, the threat of competition from Germany's European trade rivals was effectively countered through the ERM, which prevented sudden, sharp devaluations of intra-ERM exchange rates. By anchoring these currencies to the DM, the German economy maintained its share of exports and continued to accumulate trade surpluses. The growth of German exports, in turn, generated the export of capital. Historically, surplus countries become financial centres by virtue of the inherent stability of their currencies which attracts international demand as a means of payments and as a reserve asset. In the case of Germany, however, this transition was countered by the Bundesbank, which sought to prevent the DM from acting as an international reserve asset (Halevi, 1995).

Since the demise of the Bretton Woods system, the Bundesbank attempted to limit the international role of the DM. This view was motivated primarily by the deep-seated concerns over the excessive creation of liquidity if the DM were to be internationalised. In order to counter the inflationary effects of US expansionary monetary policies,

TABLE 4.1 *Comparative inflation rates between the major OECD countries, 1970–89*

Period	Germany	US	UK	Japan	France	Italy
1970–74	5.1	6.1	9.6	10.7	7.7	9.1
1975–79	4.2	8.1	15.7	7.5	10.2	15.9
1980–84	4.5	7.5	9.6	3.9	11.2	16.6
1984–89	1.3	3.6	5.3	1.2	3.6	6.2
1970–89	3.9	6.3	10.0	5.8	8.1	11.9

Source: OECD Economic Surveys, 1990.

DOI: 10.1057/9781137371904

the Bundesbank adopted monetary targeting in 1975. Informed by the prevailing monetarist doctrines, which had propounded that monetary growth impacts on the growth of national income, the rate of inflation and the nominal exchange rate, the Bundesbank pursued a low inflationary strategy to induce capital formation. As Table 4.1 highlights, Germany's anti-inflationary record was unrivalled by the major OECD countries. Given this historical credibility, other members of the ERM chose to peg their currencies to the German mark in order to acquire similar credentials as stable, low risk countries for investment and long-term capital formation.

The unwillingness of the Bundesbank to liberalise financial markets reflected this overriding objective to maintain strict control over monetary growth as the main weapon against inflation. These controls extended to restrictions on foreign bank deposits, which were required to have a higher minimum reserve ratio than resident deposits. Capital controls were also imposed on German financial institutions, which limited the issuing of DM-denominated bonds in international capital markets. Despite the liberalisation of capital markets in the mid-1980s that had abolished most of these restrictions, German capital markets still lagged behind the more sophisticated financial centres in London and New York. German capital markets continued to be quite narrow and were governed by a regime of credit-rationing, which favoured the large, industrial conglomerates, while investment outlets were dominated by the big banks that were reluctant to purchase portfolios of foreign bonds. An excellent summary of this dynamic is provided by Halevi and Kriesler:

> The reason why domestic demand is seen to be clashing with exports and the reason why export growth is privileged is to be seen in the political economy of German foreign investment and of German money. Foreign investment obviously expands the world oligopolistic power of Germany's big corporations and, unlike the American case, it is also viewed as a way to fuel German exports. The financing of this process is considered to depend upon the accumulation of German surpluses and not upon the issuing of liabilities. The German banking system de facto operates on the basis of credit rationing favoring the international investment of those companies that can pay for it via their export surpluses. (Halevi and Kriesler, 2004, p.34)

In stark contrast, D-mark Eurobonds were traded by investors outside Germany. Indeed, the demand for DM-denominated assets increased as

DOI: 10.1057/9781137371904

TABLE 4.2 *Currency distribution of foreign exchange intervention, 1979–87 (percentage of the total)*

	Intervention in the EMS		
Currency	1979–82	1983–85	1986–87
US dollars	71.5	53.7	26.3
EMS currencies	27.2	43.5	71.7
(DMs)	(23.7)	(39.4)	(59.0)
Others	1.3	2.8	2.0

Source: Commission Departments, 1988.

the process of trade interpenetration accelerated. Since a growing proportion of this trade was denominated in marks, the demand for DMs also increased. Similarly, the number of German banks operating in foreign countries had risen from only 8 in 1970 to 186 in 1988. Conversely, the number of branches of foreign banks operating in Germany had increased from 25 to 58 over the same period (Tavlas, 1991, pp.19–20). The most striking evidence of the rise in the international role of the DM, however, was in its use as an intervention currency in the ERM. As Table 4.2 demonstrates, the share of US dollar interventions declined from 71.5 per cent in 1979–82 to 26.3 per cent in 1986–87, while the share of DM interventions increased from 23.7 to 59 per cent during the same period. This evidence suggests that the US dollar was gradually replaced by the DM in intra-EMS interventions. After the liberalisation of the German capital markets in 1984–85, the international role of the DM also increased as a reserve asset and as a means of payments. Between 1980 and 1989, international DM claims in Germany increased by about 180 per cent while those held outside Germany increased by 125 per cent (Tavlas, 1991, p.31).

After the demise of the Bretton Woods system, a three key-currency configuration emerged with the rise of the DM and the Japanese yen as major reserve currencies. This new configuration reflected the portfolio preferences of investors in their desire to reduce the risks associated with the exclusive use of US dollars and the demand by creditors to diversify from dollar denominated assets. As the DM appreciated against the US dollar after 1985, long-term interest rates reflected this relationship. The fact that German long-term rates were lower than those in the US implied that the dollar was expected to continue to depreciate. International monetary stability was therefore increasingly based upon the substitution of

DOI: 10.1057/9781137371904

the three key currencies. While the US dollar continued to perform the dominant role as an international means of payments, the DM and the yen had emerged as key reserve currencies in international markets by virtue of the fact of their cumulative trade surpluses and their respective accumulation of large foreign exchange reserves.

The widening gulf between growing German trade surpluses and the trade deficits of France and Italy threatened the cohesion and stability of the EMS. Germany's trade surplus with its EMS partners increased more than four-fold between 1979 and 1988. At the same time, France's trade deficit increased more than three-fold (Table 4.3). In other words, German trade surpluses threatened to provoke a revival of national protectionism. This spectre was temporarily averted because the penetration of German exports was offset by an increase in German investment in these markets. The refusal of the German authorities to stimulate the level of effective demand, however, imparted disinflationary impulses in the EMS zone. There was a very real danger that a "depressive spiral" could be set in motion as each member state imposed highly contractionary policies and tolerated higher levels of unemployment. The "fallacy of composition" would suggest that as each country attempted to increase their exports to other member countries, these exports encountered the limits set by austerity policies enacted by each of these countries. If extra-Community markets also diminished, this depressive spiral could have degenerated into a vicious circle of competitive devaluations and "beggar thy neighbour" policies reminiscent of the 1930s. Indeed, this cumulative process of competitive disinflation has characterised the dynamics of the European economy since the late 1980s (Boltho, 1993).

Table 4.3 *Trade balance of the EMS countries, 1979–88 ($US billions/percentage of GDP)*

Country	1979	1983	1986	1987	1988
Belgium	−0.8 (0.7)	−0.8	−0.6	−0.7 (0.5)	−3.4
Denmark	−2.2 (3.4)	−1.1	−3.4	−2.8 (2.9)	−1.8
France	−7.0 (1.2)	−12.4	−17.00	−20.7 (2.3)	−21.9
Germany	5.7 (0.7)	4.1	15.4	22.3 (2.0)	26.5
Ireland	0.3 (8.1)	0.9	1.8	3.0 (24.9)	3.4
Italy	−0.9 (0.3)	−1.3	−3.4	−6.1 (0.8)	−8.6
Netherlands	4.9 (3.1)	10.6	7.3	5.0 (2.3)	5.7

Source: OECD Economic Surveys, 1990.

DOI: 10.1057/9781137371904

The extent to which the major deficit countries of France and Italy were willing to tolerate high unemployment by assigning low inflation as the cornerstone to their macroeconomic objectives ultimately determined whether the EMS was able to maintain its internal cohesion. In the absence of a reflationary policy in Germany, the deficit countries were compelled to rely on capital controls to maintain their respective exchange rate parities. This, in turn, implied that the deficit countries had to contend with overvalued exchange rates, which had the effect of distorting their domestic prices and impaired their international competitiveness. The impact of this exchange rate constraint on the ability of a deficit country to pursue an expansionary programme was graphically portrayed in France after the election of the Socialist government in 1981. Within two years, an unprecedented flight of capital had occurred, induced by a two-fold increase in the current account deficit. Over Ff80bn had fled the country as the French economy experienced a sudden quadrupling of the national debt from Ff123bn in 1980 to Ff451bn in 1983 (Petit, 1989, p.259). By early 1983, after the third successive exchange rate crisis, the Mitterrand government abandoned "Keynesianism in one country". Anti-inflationary policies were introduced to stabilise the franc and stem the outflow of capital. In the wake of these measures, the European Commission agreed to provide a loan of 4 billion ECUs to finance the current account deficit. According to Pivetti:

> In the light of these difficulties of a practical and political nature, it can be affirmed that without capital controls it is virtually impossible to preserve each state's sovereign right to choose its tax system, and that governments wanting to redistribute income from capital to labour could hardly avoid reintroducing capital controls: on the one hand, they would allow a reduction of the domestic interest rate at which the government refinances its domestic debt – and hence also the amount of revenue that the government needs to raise; on the other hand, they would facilitate the taxation of domestic capital and, more generally, wealth. (1998, p.10)

As the French case demonstrated, the survival of the EMS inevitably depended upon the ability of member countries to co-ordinate their macroeconomic policies and to pursue a convergence of national inflation rates. Germany's low inflation provided an anchor for the other ERM countries while its domestic savings financed investment in the deficit countries. Conversely, the nominal appreciation of the DM increased Germany's purchasing power over European assets. During the 1970s,

DOI: 10.1057/9781137371904

this virtuous circle was based upon the configuration of low growth and disinflation in Germany, on the one hand, and high growth and rampant inflation in France and Italy, on the other hand. Consequently, Italy and France experienced an increased penetration of German exports, thereby becoming more dependent on German investment. The continuation of this virtuous circle could be sustained only if the deficit countries could adjust externally through exchange rate devaluations. During the 1980s, membership of the ERM imposed limits on this exchange rate adjustment. The emphasis was now placed upon internal adjustment through a programme of disinflation. By independently targeting its monetary growth, Germany established the inflationary threshold to which its ERM partners aligned themselves. Average inflation in the EMS fell from about 11 per cent in 1980 to around 2 per cent in 1986 while the differentials between the highest and lowest national inflation rates had narrowed from 16 per cent to about 6 per cent (Padoa-Schioppa, 1988, p.371). Figure 4.2 illustrates this convergence of inflation rates. It should be noted that much of the success of the EMS in terms of national inflation and exchange rate convergence up until 1989 can be explained largely in light of the propitious international environment discussed in the previous chapter. The other caveat is that the main burden of adjustment was borne by the deficit countries as they experienced lower growth

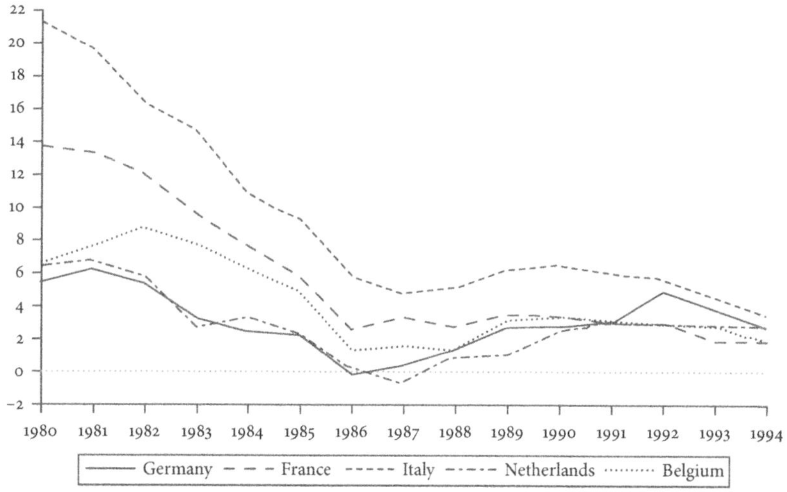

FIGURE 4.2 *Consumer Price Index (inflation rate) in selected EMS countries, 1980–94 (% pa)*

DOI: 10.1057/9781137371904

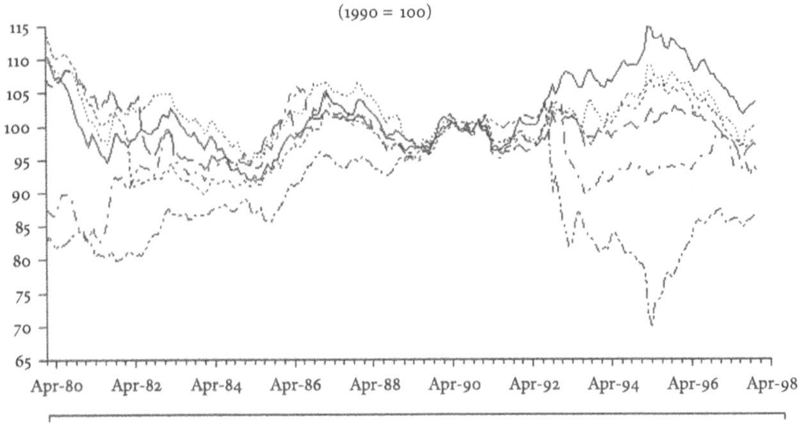

FIGURE 4.3 *Real effective exchange rates in selected EMS countries, 1980–98*

and higher unemployment. In order to prevent speculative attacks, both France and Italy imposed more stringent capital controls on the inflow of capital. Figure 4.3 illustrates the relative success in exchange rate convergence up until 1992.

With the signing of the Single European Act (SEA) in 1986, capital controls were scheduled to be abolished in 1992. Consequently, one of the main pillars of the EMS, which contributed to the stabilisation of intra-Community exchange rates, had disappeared. The liberalisation of capital movements, however, became difficult to reconcile with the continued existence of national exchange rate regimes. This glaring dichotomy became evident during the speculative turmoil that engulfed the EMS in mid-1992. The solution to this dichotomy was perceived to be the realisation of complete monetary union, which would abolish intra-EC exchange rate fluctuations with the creation of a European central bank issuing a single currency. Monetary union implied a symmetrical regime of exchange rate convergence. The EMS, however, was characterised by asymmetrical exchange rate relations with Germany acting as the nominal exchange rate anchor for the system as a whole. It was precisely this problem that informed contending national strategies over the creation of a single currency. In other words, to what extent would the demands of the German monetary authorities determine the final blueprint for EMU? Or to pose the question in a different guise: would the Bundesbank be willing to surrender its monetary autonomy?

DOI: 10.1057/9781137371904

And if so, would the institutional architecture of a European Central Bank emulate the monetarist design of the Bundesbank? The whole problem therefore reverts to the political ramifications of German economic hegemony. According to Marsh:

> The snake and EMS/ERM experiences provided backing for the economic theory of the so-called "Impossible Trinity" that gained ground during the 1980s, according to which countries could not simultaneously maintain fixed exchange rates, capital mobility and autonomous monetary policies. By the late 1980s, many European countries, either voluntarily, or with varying degrees of unwillingness, had effectively given up monetary autonomy to the Germans. (2009, pp.7–8)

A single currency?

The Brussels Council that had established the EMS in 1978 had identified the ECU as the pivot around which intra-EMS exchange rates would be expressed. The ECU would constitute the official numeraire for the ERM and the means of settlement between the central banks. From these quite modest foundations, it was envisaged that the ECU would eventually evolve into a single currency. However, the ECU was devoid of legal tender status and restrictions were imposed on its convertibility. According to Masera (1987), the limited role of official ECUs as a means of payments had stemmed from the reluctance of central banks, most notably the Bundesbank, to undertake "symmetrical" interventions which would adversely affect their respective monetary bases. In other words, compulsory interventions at the margins through the VSTF were governed by central bank swap agreements which generated the movement of reserves in both directions. This implied a contraction of the monetary bases of the weak currency countries and an expansion of the intervening strong currency countries. Unless these capital inflows were sterilised by the central bank of the latter, the growth of liquidity could induce an upsurge in inflation and excessive credit creation. As a result, most central bank interventions were voluntary and intra-marginal to prevent currency fluctuations from reaching their compulsory divergence thresholds. Quite contrary to the original EMS agreement, intra-marginal and asymmetrical interventions were the norm.

DOI: 10.1057/9781137371904

> It should be noted here that in the asymmetrical arrangement the flow of liquidity from the periphery to the centre country does not affect the money stock in the latter country. In this asymmetrical system, the centre country automatically sterilises the liquidity inflow by reverse open market operations. If it did not do so, the monetary expansion engineered by the peripheral country would lead to an increase of the money stock of the centre country. That country would then also lose its function of an anchor for the whole system. (De Grauwe, 1992, p.118)

Despite the limited use of official ECUs in the financing and intervention mechanisms of the EMS, it was impossible to impose restrictions on the growth of private ECUs. Since the process of credit creation occurred through the mechanism of the VSTF in which the participating countries of the ERM were compelled to intervene at the margins by borrowing ECUs in unlimited amounts, the growth of secondary ECUs were created by the stock of primary ECUs through the revolving swap agreements between central banks. These primary ECUs were issued in exchange for the deposit of 20 per cent of the gold and dollar reserves by the central banks with the EMCF. A rudimentary reserve structure was thus established for the expansion of official ECUs. Table 4.4 illustrates this reserve composition of the EMS between 1979 and 1985.

By 1985, private ECUs accounted for about 3 per cent of the international currency market and had risen to fifth rank in terms of the denomination of foreign bond issues (Masera, 1987, p.11). Most of this expansion was attributed to Italian and French private agents and public enterprises attracted by the lower risk premium and lower interest rates offered by ECU-denominated borrowings. The expansion of ECU-

TABLE 4.4 *Net official reserves of countries in the ERM ($US billions)*

	1979	1982	1985
Gold	77.5	86.9	80.0
Convertible currencies	55.0	36.9	58.5
(dollars)	(50.0)	(30.6)	(37.3)
(EMS currencies)	(4.3)	(4.4)	(17.4)
ECUs	38.2	37.6	35.2
Net position on:			
The IMF	10.4	11.4	12.0
Others	-6.3	-14.6	-12.1
Total	174.8	158.2	173.6

Source: Micossi, p.333.

DOI: 10.1057/9781137371904

bonds, however, accounted only for a negligible proportion of the total borrowings within the Community. In early 1985, the Committee of Central Bank Governors agreed to ease some of the restrictions imposed on official ECUs by allowing central banks outside the EMS to purchase ECUs. These operations, however, were presided over by the Bank for International Settlements and confined to temporary swap agreements. As international demand for ECUs increased, these financial instruments became more liquid, which also improved and enhanced their role as an international reserve asset. This trend was reflected in the increase in the share of total ECU issues made by foreign borrowers from about 10 per cent to 40 per cent between 1982 and 1985 (Micossi, 1985, pp.339–40). The rise of private ECUs in international markets appeared to coincide and support the "parallel currency" proposals of the "All Saints Day" manifesto announced by a group of nine prominent economists as early as November 1975 (*Economist*, 1 November '75). According to this manifesto, a single currency – the Europa – would circulate in direct competition with the existing plethora of national currencies. The market would ultimately determine whether the Europa would supersede the existing system of national currencies. A similar proposal for a parallel currency was promoted by the British alternative plan to the Delors Report in 1989 but failed to attract Community support (George, 1991, p.183). Given the inconvertibility of the ECU and its primary function as a unit of account in central bank operations, its potential status as a European currency was constrained by the absence of a European central bank.

A single European currency would doubtless foster a more equitable sharing of the burden of exchange rate adjustment between member states. In theory, a single currency would provide a more efficient means of central bank intervention. By circumventing intra-Community exchange rate fluctuations, monetary union would abolish the speculative propensities caused by short-term shifts in portfolio holdings denominated in existing national currencies. Despite these compelling economic arguments in favour of monetary union, the greatest obstacle was the reluctance of the Bundesbank to surrender its sovereignty over national monetary policies. In order to attract the support of the Bundesbank, the European Central Bank would need to mirror the policies and structure of the former. In other words, price stability would have to be assigned as the paramount objective of the ECB, while the ECB Board would have to exhibit political independence. These German

DOI: 10.1057/9781137371904

objectives, however, soon encountered French opposition. The French were strident advocates of political control over monetary policy. As the EMU project evolved, these tensions continued to reverberate and became the source of serious conflict over the political objectives that informed monetary policy.

Conclusion

The implications of German economic hegemony manifest themselves in the asymmetrical dynamics of intra-European trade and exchange rate relations. The emergence of Germany as the dominant core country of the European economy was mirrored in the concomitant rise of the DM as the nominal exchange rate anchor for the EMS. Given the German ideological preference for a low inflationary strategy, a cumulative process of competitive disinflation between ERM member states was set in motion as each country attempted to emulate the German preference for low inflationary growth. Unlike Germany, however, the weaker deficit countries could not accomplish a trade-off between economic growth and low inflation in order to promote exchange rate stability. This exchange rate constraint, however, merely exacerbated the powerful disinflationary forces within the EMS zone and contributed to an increase in unemployment. Consequently, the process of "competitive disinflation" threatened to generate a vicious circle as each country was compelled to adopt an export-led strategy of growth in order to overcome their respective balance of payments deficits. But as each country implemented policies that dampened the level of effective demand, the propensity to import was curtailed. The spectre of a "depressive spiral" was averted because German trade surpluses were accompanied by an increase in German investment in the EMS zone. Furthermore, the economic recovery of the US economy provided an expanding market for European exports.

While Germany increased its export surpluses within the EMS zone, Italy and France, in particular, experienced an increase in their respective trade deficits with Germany. This asymmetrical trade configuration emerged as a serious threat to the stability and cohesion of the EMS. In the absence of a German policy of reflation, the deficit countries experienced higher levels of unemployment. In theory, monetary union should ease these asymmetrical tensions by imposing a more equitable

DOI: 10.1057/9781137371904

sharing of the burden of structural adjustment. With the emergence of German economic dominance, however, the institutional framework of the European Central Bank would tend to reflect German ideological preferences. Indeed, the ratification of the Maastricht Treaty in 1993 had already assimilated the monetarist paradigm favoured by Germany.

Notes

1 In the early post-war years, the making of Europe was the answer to Germany's own making with the creation of supranational institutions and agreements (i.e., the European Coal and Steel Community (ECSC) in 1951 and the common market with the signing of the Rome Treaty in 1958). To paraphrase Schuman – one of the central architects of the post-war peace settlement – the object of Franco-German rapprochement was "To make war not only unthinkable but materially impossible".

2 An estimated 75 per cent of German exports were destined to Europe in the 1990s, while EU members received about two thirds (Bibow, 2012, p.21).

3 There is considerable evidence to support the Kaleckian proposition that an increase in the profit share of national income causes chronic problems of excess productive capacity in the absence of a concomitant increase in real wages. As long as real wages lag behind productivity growth, the problem of a severe lack of effective demand will persist. In Germany, this problem of *realisation* was temporarily resolved through a mercantilistic policy of increasing trade surpluses (Kalecki, 1969). A more detailed exposition of this Kaleckian dynamic is developed in Chapter 7.

DOI: 10.1057/9781137371904

5

Project 1992

Abstract: *In the aftermath of the second oil price shocks of 1978–79, the economies of the EC-12 experienced the most severe recession since the reconversion crisis of 1947–48. Although the recession was international in its scope, its severity and duration were greater in the EC-12 than in the US and Japan. Within five years, unemployment had doubled. Indeed, since the mid-1970s, the phenomena of what was euphemistically described as the onset of "Eurosclerosis" – the combination of high unemployment and low economic growth – had pervaded the economic landscape. Project 1992 was formulated as a neoliberal solution the Europe's perceived lack of dynamism and loss of export competitiveness.*

Lucarelli, Bill. *Endgame for the Euro: A Critical History.* Basingtoke: Palgrave Macmillan, 2013.
DOI: 10.1057/9781137371904.

 DOI: 10.1057/9781137371904

Introduction

Although the recession was international in its scope, its severity and duration were greater in the EC-12 than in the US and Japan. Between 1974 and 1985, the economies of the EC-12 had been outperformed by their international rivals in Japan and the United States. While Community economic growth had averaged only 1.9 per cent per annum during this period, the US and Japan had experienced an average of 2.4 and 3.8 per cent respectively. Similarly, inflation in the EC-12 stood at an average of 11 per cent compared with 7 per cent in the US and 6.3 per cent in Japan over the same period.

Between 1973 and 1985, intra-Community trade had stagnated and declined in some sectors. The trade-creating dynamics of the Common Market had therefore ceased to provide a catalyst in the process of economic integration. To be sure, with the decline in the volume of world trade after the first oil price shocks, the European customs union had begun to resemble the caricature portrayed by its critics as "fortress Europe". The crisis of excess capacity in the shipbuilding, steel, textile and car industries had culminated in the imposition of import quotas, state aid and indirect tariff restrictions by national governments, which threatened to develop into destructive intra-EC trade wars. The causes of this crisis were the subject of perennial debates centred on the structural weaknesses of Europe's industry and the growing perception that the continent had fallen behind their competitors in their traditional markets and in the strategic high technology sectors. This was reflected most strikingly in the increased penetration of European markets by American and Japanese transnational corporations in the automobile and electronics sectors.

The neoliberal ascendancy

By the early 1980s, problems of severe excess capacity and growing income inequalities manifested themselves in a general crisis of over-accumulation. The falling rate of profit experienced during the 1970s and early 1980s was eventually counteracted and reversed by the 1990s through the repression of wages and sustained by the phenomenon of "financialisation." The fall in the wages share of national income was necessary to reverse the tendency toward falling profitability (Dumenil

DOI: 10.1057/9781137371904

and Levy, 1993). However, the restoration of profitability inevitably encountered the limits set by the chronic lack of effective demand (Lucarelli, 2011). In most European countries, income inequalities only worsened over time as real wages stagnated. Real purchasing power was increasingly augmented by burgeoning levels of household debt (Barba and Pivetti, 2009, p.122). Instead of providing the foundations for technological reconversion and industrial upgrading, the sharp increases in aggregate profits were dissipated into corporate mergers and acquisitions, speculative financial engineering, and other forms of rent-seeking and entirely fictitious forms of capital. In the aftermath of financial deregulation in the early 1980s, these speculative propensities reached truly astounding proportions and led to an unprecedented series of asset price booms.

The lack of effective demand led to the growth of excess liquidity, which was increasingly channelled into the financial markets and financed burgeoning levels of debt, which in turn supported hyper-excessive private consumption and generated recurrent asset-price booms. Similarly, the perverse "wealth effects" induced by this type of financial leverage set in motion a negative feedback loop, which further reinforced the vicious circle of debt-financed consumption and asset-price inflation. The stagnation of real wages during the neoliberal era witnessed an increase in private indebtedness as workers resorted more than ever to the lure of credit in order to maintain their purchasing power (Dumenil and Levy, 2004, p.84). Wage repression was accompanied by growing income inequalities and greater job insecurities with the growth of casualised and more precarious forms of low wage employment. These negative trends had the overall effect of dampening the level of effective demand, which put more pressure on government spending as the automatic stabilisers were considerably weakened by the neoliberal ideological obsession for small government and the doctrine of "sound finance".

Financialisation was governed by the transformation of future streams of income (profit, dividends, and interest) into marketable and traded assets in the form of equities or bonds. In other words, financialisation represented a profound shift away from direct investment in productive capacity, towards the open financial markets in which profitability could be temporarily boosted through speculative operations in the stock markets. Shareholder value was temporarily bolstered in the short term by corporate mergers and acquisitions or through equity buy-backs. The whole logic of subjecting corporate profitability to the short-term

DOI: 10.1057/9781137371904

valuation of the stock market in order to maximise shareholder returns was a response to the profitability crisis in the 1970s and 1980s (Dumenil and Levy, 2004). Confronted by a profit squeeze and rising capital–output ratios as a result of persistent and chronic problems of excess capacity, non-financial firms were compelled to restore profitability not only through wage repression but also by diverting investment into the financial and equity markets (Krippner 2005, p.182). To be sure, under the conditions of depressed profitability, non-financial firms were reluctant to increase productive capacity in the face of an intensification of price competition and saturated markets (Bramble 2009, p.51). It can be surmised that financialisation merely postponed the impending structural problem of falling profitability.

The ascendancy of a finance-led regime of accumulation therefore involved a shift away from the normal strategy of ploughing back profits into long-term investment, towards the short-term strategy of purchasing financial assets and bolstering shareholder value. In other words, as Lazonick and O'Sullivan have argued, there was a shift from the previous "Fordist" model of "retain and invest" to a finance-led strategy of "downsize and distribute" (Lazonick and O'Sullivan, 2000). The recycling of distributed profits into capital markets, however, generated a powerful unintended consequence. As the demand for tradeable financial assets exploded, a long-term inflationary tendency was experienced in asset prices. In this speculative dynamic, higher asset prices relative to the prices of current output only served to lower the margins of safety built into bank lending. Greater financial leverage in turn spurred higher asset prices. This whole process of debt-financed speculation increased the degree of financial instability (Minsky, 1982).

The policies of financial deregulation, privatisation and greater labour market flexibility advocated by the new neoliberal consensus soon gained the ascendancy over the previous Keynesian policies of national demand management and "financial repression." Unleashed from the constraints imposed by national regimes of regulation, the neoliberal policies favoured by the proponents of the single market promoted the rise of finance capital. In this sense, the new monetarist orthodoxy signified the "revenge of the rentier" as the imposition of anti-inflationary policies sought to restore the value of financial assets from the depredations of inflation and inflationary expectations caused by the series of oil-price shocks during the 1970s and 1980s. The policies of "sound finance," which implied a curtailment of public spending and a return to the pre-

DOI: 10.1057/9781137371904

Keynesian doctrine of balanced government budgets, was instrumental in reversing the post-war political consensus over the maintenance of full employment. The neoliberal proponents of "sound finance" pursued policies of financial deregulation in order to discipline so-called profligate governments to pursue policies of fiscal consolidation. National fiscal policies were now subjected to the vagaries of bond markets.

From the standpoint of the neoliberal paradigm, the prevailing national regimes of accumulation had exhausted themselves. The crisis of overcapacity and economic stagnation had exposed the limits of these national strategies which had been governed by the "social market" policies of both the Christian Democrats and Social Democratic coalitions. Neoliberal critics argued that these national policies could no longer be legitimised. This ideological shift away from the prevailing corporatist forms of state regulation (i.e., the welfare state, Keynesianism and industry intervention) coincided with the demands of transnational corporations based in Europe that these national modes of regulation and protectionism should be gradually abolished. National deregulation, privatisation of public corporations and market liberalisation became the neoliberal mantra. The removal of non-tariff barriers, the opening up of public procurement policies and liberalisation of capital markets also conformed to these transnational objectives. Most of these ostensible "efficiency" gains would be secured through cost reductions and rationalisation in order to promote greater economies of scale and improve competitiveness. The neoliberal strategy not only implied the dismantling of national modes of regulation but the curbing of the power of organised labour in order to foster greater labour market flexibility and mobility. Indeed, it was precisely the objective of restoring profitability by reducing the wages share of national income through the classical mechanism of the reserve army of unemployed labour, which informed the neoliberal strategy of economic restructuring in favour of capital. With the labour movement on the defensive, the hegemony of capital was restored (Harvey, 2006).

The neoliberal ascendancy was reflected in a general shift to political right within the EC during the 1980s, regardless of the ideological persuasion of the respective political parties in power. This was most evident in France after the abandonment of "Keynesianism in one country" by the Socialist government in 1983. Similarly, the Spanish Socialists pursued neoliberal policies after their election in 1981. Given this political configuration, the Thatcher government in the UK found it quite propitious

DOI: 10.1057/9781137371904

to support the single market proposals despite opposition to institutional and procedural reforms embodied by the principle of majority voting in the Council of Ministers and the European Social Charter. The political agenda of the Community was therefore dominated by the governments in power in the northern industrial "core" countries of France, Germany and the UK. This favourable political configuration made it possible for a recasting of the European bargain towards a neoliberal direction (Grahl and Teague, 1989). Even before the official ratification of the Single European Act, European big business had been mobilising support in the European Commission to adopt a neoliberal solution to the lack of economic dynamism and growth. These demands coalesced in the Rountable of European Industrialists, an organisation represented by Europe's most powerful corporations, including Phillips, Siemens, Olivetti, Fiat, GEC, Daimler Benz, Volvo, ASEA, Bosch and Ciba-Geigy. One of the architects of this elite group was the Commissioner for Industry, Etienne Davignon. An elite alliance soon emerged between transnational business interests and the European Commission, which culminated in the election of Delors to the Presidency of the Commission in early 1985 (Moravcsik, 1991).

The process of inter-state bargaining over the proposals of the SEA was launched during the European Council Summit at Fontainbleau in June 1984. From this Summit, the Doogue Committee was established and chaired by Lord Cockfield, who was the British Commissioner for Trade and Industry. It was from this Committee that the final SEA White Paper entitled "The Completion of the Internal Market" was presented to the Council at the Luxembourg Summit in March 1985 (George, 1991, p.160). A few months later in Brussels, the Council agreed to a timetable for the 279 proposals to be implemented by December 1992. By the end of the year, the SEA was officially ratified by the Council and signed by the 12 member states in February 1986. The legislation eventually came into legal force in July 1987 after referenda were held in Denmark and Ireland (Tsoukalis, 1993, p.61).

The process of economic and legal harmonisation would be accompanied by the introduction of majority voting in the Council of Ministers (Article 100a) in order to allow the passage of the SEA legislation to be adopted more easily. The only exceptions involved agreements over capital liberalisation and treaties governing air and sea transport. Consequently, the SEA linked the liberalisation of the internal market with procedural reform. The Luxembourg Compromise of 1967, which had enshrined the

DOI: 10.1057/9781137371904

powers of national veto over Community legislation was temporarily suspended.[1] Community constitutional and legal prerogatives, however, were merely confined to legislation related to the SEA. In this crucial sense, the SEA embraced a much wider agenda to include increased powers of the European parliament, social cohesion and collaboration in research and development. The Social Action Programme involved over 50 measures, which covered the free movement of labour within the Community, the basic wage, training and associated health, safety and other working conditions. Although the financial contribution to the structural funds was doubled, the Social Charter encountered quite staunch opposition from the Thatcher government, which regarded these proposals as ideological anathema.

The initiative for political reform originated from the "Crocodile Club", which was composed of the most prominent supporters of the federalist cause. One of its leaders, Altierio Spinelli,[2] was instrumental in formulating the resolution in the European parliament, which established the draft treaty for European political union as early as July 1981. The draft treaty was adopted by an overwhelming majority of the European Parliament (EP) in February 1984. One of the central pillars was the principle of "subsidiarity" which informed the Maastricht Treaty in 1992. In other words, common action between member states would require a majority vote whereas unanimity would apply to the more sensitive political agreements (Wistrich, 1989, pp.38–39).

At the Milan Summit meeting in June 1985, an intergovernmental conference was established to discuss political and procedural reforms. These discussions culminated in the procedural reforms embodied in the SEA. The European Parliament would be given greater legislative powers to amend Council proposals. If the EP's amendments were accepted by the Commission, then the Council could reject these amendments only by a unanimous vote whereas only a majority vote was required by the Council to accept these amendments (Daltrop, 1992, p.91). Similarly, the applications for EC membership and association agreements with third countries were now subject to parliamentary approval (Wistrich, 1989, p.9). Although the executive powers of the Council of Ministers remained intact, these procedural reforms signalled a willingness to increase the legislative powers of the EP. The SEA also enshrined formal legal status to the European Political Co-operation (EPC) in the formulation of a common foreign policy and the informal summit meetings between the 12 European government leaders (Nugent, 1991, p.36).

DOI: 10.1057/9781137371904

The neoliberal strategy was therefore accompanied by a set of policy-led initiatives. Despite British opposition, Delors had sought to complement these deregulatory measures on the national level with new forms of regulation on the supranational level. The application of "competition among rules" governed these policy initiatives (Woolcock, *et al.*, 1991, p.9). Delors's vision encompassed a European "organised space" between the nation-state and the global market. It was envisaged that Europe would become the organising centre of a regional regulatory bloc to counter the destabilising forces of globalisation (Ross, 1992, p.62). The neoliberal strategy was informed by the overwhelming imperative to improve Europe's competitiveness in the global market. With the publication of the influential Cecchini Report in 1988, a blueprint for this strategy had been sketched out.

According to the Cecchini Report, the economic benefits of the SEA were estimated at about 6 per cent of the Community GDP (Cecchini, 1988). In retrospect, these estimates were quite optimistic. The more heroic assumptions could be identified with the neoliberal faith in the efficacy of the market. The basic theoretical contention was that market liberalisation would generate an increase in the level of productive investment and economic restructuring through the purgative forces induced by competition. Moreover these competitive forces would ostensibly foster a rapid upsurge in the rate of corporate mergers and promote greater economies of scale and increased returns to scale as firms integrated their operations across national borders. The whole strategy hinged on the dismantling of national forms of capitalist regulation and state support for "national champions". The fatal flaw of the neoliberal programme, however, was the absence of corresponding regimes of regulation on the supranational level. This was especially evident in the relatively minor role performed by the European budget as a redistributive mechanism and the very limited development of coherent Community state structures and institutions.

The Single Market Programme also reflected dramatic changes in international geo-political alignments. With the relative demise of the post-war system of *Pax Americana*, the single market emerged as a regional organising centre of the emergent multi-polar system of economic blocs. This redivision of the world market was accompanied by the disintegration of the Soviet bloc. As a result of these dramatic post-Cold War re-alignments, the Community's international relations were transformed beyond recognition. In contrast to its former role as a

DOI: 10.1057/9781137371904

strategic bulwark against the Soviet Union, the Community became the new focus or "centre" to which the newly emergent capitalist countries of eastern Europe gravitated. After the collapse of the Soviet bloc in eastern Europe in 1989, the US defence umbrella of NATO had lost its *raison d'etre.* A more independent defence and foreign policy was now possible.

After German re-unification, support for closer European co-operation was perceived as a necessary corollary in order to incorporate the former East German socialist state. At the same time, the prospect of potential export markets and investment in eastern Europe had rekindled Germany's traditional economic dominance of this region (Spaulding, 1991). In this sense, the former socialist countries now emerged as candidates for EC membership. The existing EC-12 thus evolved as the core of a system of concentric circles with the European Free Trade Association (EFTA)[3] countries and the former socialist countries gravitating as satellite states around this "core". Although the Franco-German accord continued to govern the political dynamics of the pan-European project, the inter-state bargaining process was modified substantially with the engagement of the UK and the other new member states. According to Eichengreen:

> At the start of the 1990s there was Germany's need to gain French assent to Germany's reunification, for which it could offer monetary union as a quid pro quo. Subsequently there was the wish in reunified Germany for a more assertive foreign policy, which could be pursued only in the context of a more deeply integrated European Union. In France there was the desire to wrest monetary control from a German central bank that dictated policy Europe-wide. The French, in the Gaullist tradition, also wanted a European currency that could rival the dollar. They valued monetary power for the same reasons they valued military power. They sought less dependence on the US monetarily as well as militarily. The euro was their monetary *force de frappe*. (2011, p.71)

Both Kohl and Mitterrand viewed Project 1992 as a catalyst in revitalising the European project after more than a decade of stagnation and political inertia. Indeed, the political timing proved to be almost uncanny since it coincided with an economic resurgence in the late 1980s. As the mini-boom gained momentum, the political climate changed from one of a pervasive "Euro-pessimism" to an excessive optimism. The euphoria became self-fulfilling. Despite the Thatcher government's opposition to elements of procedural reform embodied in the SEA, the perennial disputes over British financial contributions to the EC budget and

DOI: 10.1057/9781137371904

ideological opposition to the Social Charter, support for the SEA was assured by the potential benefits that British financial institutions could derive with the liberalisation of financial markets. It was the dynamism of the Commission, led by the skilful political talents of Delors, which provided a new impetus in the revival of the neo-functionalist "snowball" effect.[4]

The regional dimension

From a historical perspective, capital accumulation has been governed by the law of uneven development. The spatial dimension of economic development has been characterised by a core/periphery configuration. One of the seminal theories of this process of circular and cumulative causation was developed by Myrdal, who argued that capital movements tend to increase regional inequality by concentrating in the more developed regions (1957). These are identified as the centrifugal, "spread effects" caused by economic expansion in the core regions which diffuse technology, capital investment and a modern infrastructure to the outlying, less developed hinterlands: "In the centres of expansion, increased demand will spur investment, which in turn will increase incomes and demand and cause a second round of investment and so on. Saving will increase as a result of higher incomes but will tend to lag behind investment in the sense that the supply of capital will steadily meet the brisk demand for it" (Myrdal, 1957, p.28). However, the opposite logic of cumulative causation is evident in the less developed regions. These are identified as the "backwash effects" which merely reinforce the structural and socio-economic disadvantages of these regions.

Capital will tend to migrate from the less profitable to the more profitable sectors and regions of a spatially defined economy. According to Emmanuel, if labour remains relatively immobile, wages in the more technically advanced sectors of the economy will be generally higher than those in the less developed regions: "Since equivalence in capitalist production relations signifies not the exchange of equal quantities of labour, but that of equal aggregates of factors (labour and the use of capital), non-equivalence (unequal exchange) can only signify the exchange of unequal aggregates of the same factors" (Emmanuel, 1972, p.325). Uneven development can therefore be defined as a sectoral disparity between different regions/countries, which exhibit differing capital/labour ratios. A dualism has evolved between the high wage, high productivity regions/countries, on the one hand, and the low wage, low productivity regions/countries, on the other hand. With the emergence of a frontier-less Europe, this process of uneven development has increased these regional disparities. As national barriers were abolished, capital became more mobile. Footloose investment intensified competition between different regions in their struggle to attract new investment. In this environment of increased competition and rationalisation, the core regions benefited at the expense of the less favoured regions. The latter competed against each other to attract the lower skilled, assembly operations by offering relatively cheaper wages.

Within Europe, uneven development has historically manifested itself in a hierarchical pattern organised along three distinct social formations. In the official EU literature on regional policy, these three social formations more or less correspond with the backward agricultural regions, the declining and depressed industrial sectors and the technologically advanced, capital intensive metropolitan centres (Padoa-Schioppa, 1987). The poorer, less developed regions are located in Southern Italy, most of Greece, Portugal, Ireland and Spain (excluding the industrial eastern provinces) where average income was less than 70 per cent of the Community average. With the accession of Spain, Portugal and Greece in the 1980s, the Community GDP increased by 10 per cent but population rose by 22 per cent and employment in agriculture increased by 57 per cent (Padoa-Schioppa, 1987, p.162). The newly emergent peripheral capitalist states of eastern Europe have also evolved as new sources of investment and cheap labour.

Given the low levels of income and employment in these less developed regions, their potential as markets has been quite limited. Since the propensity to save has been relatively low, local investment was insufficient to generate a self-sustaining phase of cumulative growth, thus reinforcing the vicious circle of poverty. As the chill winds of competition induced by market liberalisation have imperilled existing enterprises and incomes, the "backwash" effects have also been reinforced. Locational disadvantages deterred investment as large firms took advantage of the single European market by improving their vertical integration and concentrating their core activities in the more lucrative markets. The more distant a market, the less likely it was to attract private investment, while the lack of a modern infrastructure in these regions further accentuated existing competitive and locational disadvantages. The

DOI: 10.1057/9781137371904

declining industrial regions were more difficult to categorise or identify. In general, these regions were associated with the more mature industrial sectors in the steel, shipbuilding and textile industries. The official criteria for identifying these regions was by classifying them in the 70 to 100 per cent range of income per head of the Community average or by identifying the above average unemployment rates. According to these criteria, more than 10 per cent of the Community population lived in these depressed regions which were located in the north and west of the UK, in the north of Spain, eastern Belgium, and in the north and east of France. Although in a state of decline and undergoing profound structural change, these industrial regions continued to augment and provide essential inputs to the more efficient, higher value-added and capital intensive manufacturing sectors. The steel industry, for instance, still provides backward linkages to the engineering and capital goods sectors.

Uneven development has emerged as one of the most critical issues for the EU authorities. Historically, industrial concentration has developed within a triangular region between Paris, Frankfurt and Milan. The original Rome treaties recognised this regional dimension, most notably in the Italian *Mezzogiorno* and established the European Investment Bank (EIB) to promote economic development in these regions. The Agricultural Guidance section of the Common Agricultural Policy was also created to encourage agricultural restructuring and the development of social and physical infrastructure. These earlier programmes, however, were merely the outcome of specific national compromises and competing national claims. After the first enlargement in the 1970s, the whole issue of regional development acquired greater impetus with the creation of the European Regional Development Fund (ERDF). The total amount of resources devoted to regional and redistributive policies, however, remained quite small compared with the expenditure assigned to these programmes by national governments. A new strategy on regional policy was launched as a central plank of the Internal Market Programme in 1985. This strategy coincided with the second enlargement of the Iberian peninsula and Greece. Its main contribution was the implementation of the Integrated Mediterranean Programmes (IMPs). In February 1988 the Council of Ministers approved a doubling of the resources to the three major regional funds.

The impact of monetary union on these less developed regions has been quite deleterious. Since labour continues to be relatively immobile

DOI: 10.1057/9781137371904

but capital has been highly mobile, wage levels have diverged between different regions. Capital has migrated to the more profitable regions, attracted by the high levels of demand and the close proximity to expanding markets. In the absence of national exchange rate policy instruments to adjust to an adverse terms of trade, monetary union has effectively transformed balance of payments crises into regional problems. The less favoured regions/countries have become more vulnerable to cost-push inflation caused by a shift in demand to the more prosperous regions/countries. As national regimes of regulation were gradually abolished, the competitiveness of these regions experienced a secular decline. At the same time, the recycling of surpluses from the metropolitan core regions to the less developed hinterlands through the Community budget has not been sufficient to offset the adverse structural impact caused by monetary union. Quite simply, the redistributive powers and the limited fiscal resources of the EU budget failed to perform this role on the required scale and scope. Despite the reform of the structural funds, these redistributive mechanisms have not been sufficient to stabilise, let alone reverse the negative effects of uneven development on these less developed regions. Although some of the less developed regions have benefited from the creation of production bases attracted by lower real wages and lower costs of production, the vast majority of these regions have been condemned to a perennial state of economic stagnation. In other words, the "backwash" effects continued to prevail over the "spill-over" effects.

A European social space?

Given the prevailing doctrines of "negative integration" that have informed the Rome treaties and the subsequent evolution of the Common Market, social policies have played only a minor role in the formulation of economic policies on the supranational level. Much of the earlier social legislation was inherited from the European Coal and Steel Community (ECSC) (Article 56), which involved the creation of a Social Fund on a 50–50 basis with national governments to assist in the resettlement of workers from declining industrial regions and contribute to education and re-training (Shanks, 1977). Social policy is enshrined in Articles 117 and 118 of the Treaty of Rome. While Articles 117–118 relate to the agreements by member states to improve working conditions, Articles 123–128 provide the statutory basis for the Social Fund. Furthermore, the freedom of movement of labour within the customs union constitutes one of the main pillars of the Treaty. These provisions are enshrined in Articles 48–58 of the Rome Treaty (Tsoukalis, 1993, p.150).

In the course of the negotiations over the first enlargement at the Hague Summit in 1969, social policy was given a more prominent status. This culminated in the Social Action Programme adopted in 1974, which comprised a rather incoherent and disparate set of policies to promote employment in the more depressed regions, worker participation in management decisions and greater consultation with the Social and Economic Committees of the Community. These measures, however, were destined to have very little impact in the face of rising unemployment and the unwillingness of national governments to contribute to the Community budget. These constraints prevented the formulation of a more coherent social policy. Social policy continued to be informed by the principles of negative integration and the prevailing neoliberal strategies which focused on the priorities of the free movement of labour and the equalisation of competitive conditions between enterprises within the customs union (Shanks, 1977, p.13).

With the second enlargement of Greece and the Iberian peninsula during the 1980s, social policy was once again given a new impetus. By 1986 about 7 per cent of the Community budget was devoted to the Social Fund, which represented a five-fold increase over the previous decade (Wistrich, 1989, p.69). In May 1989 the Commission produced the first draft of a Social Charter as part of the Internal Market Programme. Despite some modifications and a dilution of its social objectives in the face of British opposition, the second draft failed to reverse these strident British objections. Delors had identified three main areas in the creation of a European "social space": (1) a charter of social rights, (2) statutory obligations for workers' participation in management and (3) fostering a dialogue between capital and labour on a European level (Tsoukalis, 1993, p.156). This progressive vision encountered hostile British Tory opposition. The eventual outcome witnessed an unprecedented scenario in which the other 11 member states signed a separate social protocol at the Strasbourg Summit in December 1989. The Social Charter formed the basis of the Social Chapter of the Maastricht Treaty signed in December 1991 and ratified by all of the member states, with the exception of Britain, in 1993. Under Article 118 of this Treaty, the

DOI: 10.1057/9781137371904

Community can legislate by a qualified majority vote on issues of health and safety, employment conditions and equal employment opportunity principles. Unanimity, however, was required for legislation covering worker participation, social security and the social protection of workers (Tsoukalis, 1993, p.172).

European trade unions, represented by the European Trade Union Confederation (ETUC), held quite legitimate reservations about the social consequences of the neoliberal strategy. Their greatest concern was the possible emergence of "social dumping" in the event of the removal of barriers on intra-European investment and competition. There was an explicit danger that firms would exploit lower wages and working conditions in the less developed regions in order to undermine established wages, conditions and fundamental labour rights in the Community as a whole. It was in this context that the first draft of the Social Charter had sought to harmonise wages and social security provisions across the EC. Confronted by hostile British opposition, however, the proposals were diluted and became a mere statement of intent, devoid of any real legislative imperatives (George, 1991, p.207). As a result of British opposition, the Social Charter was largely symbolic. Articles 100a and 118a of the SEA enshrined legislation to improve and harmonise national standards of health and safety, environmental laws and consumer protection. The need to compensate those regions and social groups that would be adversely affected by economic restructuring was enshrined in Articles 130a and 130b of the SEA, which commits the EC to strengthen social cohesion through the regional and structural funds, including the Social Fund. Beyond these measures, it is evident that the neoliberal strategy has prevailed by confining the social dimension of the Internal Market Programme to the issues of labour mobility and minimal regulation on a European level. The final draft of the Social Charter was devoid of any legal force and had become nothing more than an act of symbolism.

Conclusion

The restoration of the competitive dynamism of European capitalism through the purgative forces generated by the neoliberal strategy has failed to materialise. Indeed, quite the contrary: in the wake of the recent sovereign debt crises that have enveloped the peripheral, deficit countries, the whole neoliberal paradigm has encountered widespread, hostile

DOI: 10.1057/9781137371904

opposition, most notably by a resurgent labour movement. Throughout the history of capitalism, the role of the state in the maintenance of social and political cohesion and mediating between competing class and sectoral interests has been absolutely essential in the reproduction of capitalist social relations. Whether this role corresponds with the nation-state or with supranational forms of regulation, state intervention has been quite central in the management of the business cycle through traditional Keynesian policies of fiscal stabilisation and redistribution. But the neoliberal strategy has threatened to abolish existing national modes of regulation without producing a coherent regulatory regime on the supranational level. Confronted by an intensification of global oligopolistic competition, European firms could resort to protectionist demands from their respective national governments. The whole dilemma therefore reduces itself to the basic contradiction between the survival of existing national regimes of accumulation, on the one hand, and the growing demands by European MNCs to decompose these structures and create a unified European "domestic" market, on the other.

Project 1992 was imbued with the nostalgia of the neo-functionalist logic of "negative integration" that had informed Europe's earlier post-war institutions and agreements (Milward, 1992, pp.441–42). In order to resolve the perceived lack of competitive dynamism, the liberal economic paradigm was re-invented. This project was accomplished in the background of momentous historical events in the former Soviet bloc. In this post-Cold War era, the emergence of a regulated economic bloc in Europe represented the more advanced expression of the new multi-polar world system of economic relations. In this overall configuration, the United States and East Asia constituted the other two global poles of capital accumulation. From this perspective, Delors's vision of a European "organised space" in the emerging world of globalised capital marked an important historical watershed. The extent to which the peripheral states of southern Europe and the newly emergent capitalist countries of eastern Europe would be accommodated in the event of monetary union, however, remained unresolved.

Notes

1 Conflict over the financing of the Community budget dominated the Community's political agenda in the 1960s. From the very outset, de Gaulle

had opposed proposals to establish an independent Community budget rather than relying on the financial contributions of member states. De Gaulle continued to oppose Community "own resources" on the grounds that it would constitute a threat to national sovereignty over fiscal policies. With the formation of the customs union, it was envisaged by the Rome Treaty (Article 205) that revenue accrued from the Common External Tariff (CET) would provide the financial base for a Community budget. The Commission would be endowed with legislative powers to frame the budget while its adoption would be the prerogative of the Council of Ministers. This would coincide with the introduction of qualified majority voting in the Council. Monnet and earlier federalists had proposed that the Community should possess its own budget in order to prevent individual member states from withdrawing their financial contributions and sabotaging Community resources. The issue of "own resources" was therefore closely interwoven with federalist aims. These federalist aims were, doubtless, anathema to de Gaulle's vision of Europe. This political impasse culminated in the withdrawal of French Ministers from the Council in July 1965 in what became known as the "empty chair" policy. As a result, the Community was thrown into disarray. By January 1966 de Gaulle was obliged to abandon this policy in favour of a political compromise. After a series of negotiations, the principle of qualified majority voting in the Council was modified to apply only to technical rather than political issues. The famous "Luxembourg Compromise" re-affirmed France's right of veto in the Council while the issue of parliamentary powers over the budget was postponed.

2 Spinelli was one of the founding members of the federalist cause during the early post-war years of European reconstruction. The federalist manifesto demanded that political union and direct elections for a European parliament should precede economic union. In Spinelli's own words: "The federalists ask that the political institutions of a democratic Europe be constructed first, taking certain powers of initiative, deliberation, decision and execution from the national executives, parliaments and judiciary. The institutions would derive their legitimacy from the consent directly expressed by European citizens without interference from the Member States in matters of federal competence. Their models are like Switzerland and the great United States." (Spinelli, 1966, p.11)

3 The UK initiated negotiations with the six non-EEC members of Switzerland, Austria, Portugal, Sweden, Norway and Denmark to form the European Free Trade Association (EFTA) in July 1959. In an obvious challenge to the Common Market, the EFTA agreed to reduce tariffs on industrial goods by an average twenty per cent in July 1960 and to abolish all tariffs and quotas within ten years. The EFTA was not recognised by the EEC authorities who preferred to negotiate with each individual member state. Regardless

DOI: 10.1057/9781137371904

of British intentions, the EFTA was never in a position to challenge the Common Market, given the comparative size of their internal market. Indeed, despite the existence of trade barriers, the continental members of the EFTA gravitated toward West Germany.

4 The post-war functionalist strategy of "negative integration" had informed Europe's earlier progress toward greater economic integration, embodied by the creation of supranational agencies and agreements such as the European Coal and Steel Community (ECSC) in 1952 and the signing of the Rome Treaties in 1958, which established the European Common Market. The functionalists advocated a gradualist strategy, which had envisaged the formation of supranational administrative regimes that would foster co-operation between nation-states and through the cumulative logic of a "spill-over" effect, would eventually lead to the surrender of national sovereignty over specific sectors of economic management. In other words, as national governments agreed to relinquish specific administrative agencies and policies to a supranational organisation, a cumulative logic would be set in motion which would expand the sphere of supranational prerogatives over other sectors.

DOI: 10.1057/9781137371904

6
The Maastricht Blueprint for EMU

Abstract: *The Maastricht Treaty represented the crowning of the edifice of the Single European Act (SEA). Despite its turbulent and difficult passage, the treaty was finally ratified by member states, with the exception of Denmark, in January 1993. The treaty embodied a revision of the Rome treaties and enshrined the objective of monetary union in the Community's protocols and principles.. The most innovative aspect of the treaty was the protocol on the Statute of the European System of Central Banks (ESCB), which enshrined the objective of monetary union. In this chapter, the strategy adopted by the Maastricht Treaty towards EMU will be critically examined.*

Lucarelli, Bill. *Endgame for the Euro: A Critical History.* Basingtoke: Palgrave Macmillan, 2013.
DOI: 10.1057/9781137371904.

 DOI: 10.1057/9781137371904

Introduction

The Maastricht Treaty represented the crowning of the edifice of the Single European Act. Despite its turbulent and difficult passage, the treaty was finally ratified by member states, with the exception of Denmark, in January 1993. The treaty embodied a revision of the Rome treaties and enshrined the objective of monetary union in the Community's protocols and principles. The two central tenets of the Treaty were informed by the principles of "subsidiarity" and "parallelism". Subsidiarity simply stated that those economic policy functions that could be more effectively enacted by the Community should be transferred from the national level. Parallelism referred to a balance in the Community's economic policies between the three main branches of public policy – allocation, stabilisation and redistribution – in order to promote greater economic integration and cohesion. The most innovative aspect of the treaty was the protocol on the Statute of the European System of Central Banks, which enshrined the objective of monetary union. In this chapter, the strategy adopted by the Maastricht Treaty toward EMU will be critically examined. The focus will be on the efficacy of the "convergence criteria" imposed on member states in order to qualify for membership of the final phase of EMU. The economic ramifications of this process of "competitive disinflation" will be highlighted to reveal its impact on the more vulnerable, peripheral deficit countries. Similarly, the question of fiscal federalism will also be examined to assess the ability of this supranational regime to perform the economic functions of re-distribution and stabilisation.

The Delors plan

In June 1988 the European Council meeting in Hanover established the Committee for the Study of Economic and Monetary Union under the chairmanship of Delors. The Delors Report, submitted in April 1989 and ratified by the member states at the Rome Summit in October 1990, provided the blueprint for monetary union. There were many close similarities with the Werner Report of the early 1970s, most notably in the liberalisation of capital markets, the irrevocable locking of exchange rates, the centralisation of monetary policy and the creation of a single European currency. The Delors plan viewed the existing EMS

DOI: 10.1057/9781137371904

architecture as the institutional foundation for the completion of the monetary edifice.

The Maastricht Treaty established a formal timetable for the progressive stages set out by the Delors Report toward EMU. The treaty also identified and elaborated on the "convergence criteria" required to qualify for membership of the final phase and the charter for a European Central Bank. Monetary union was to be accomplished through three progressive stages. During the first stage, which officially began on 1 July 1990, the EMS member states were scheduled to abolish all existing capital controls on the movement of capital across national borders. In order to prevent a speculative attack, the degree of exchange rate convergence and surveillance between central banks was strengthened. In December 1991, an agreement to establish the ECB was ratified even though exchange rate re-alignments were still permitted. The second stage was launched on 1 January 1994 with the creation of the European Monetary Institute (EMI) which prepared the groundwork for a more cohesive regime of central bank co-ordination. However, the EMI was not assigned any real powers to act as a de facto central bank but merely monitored progress on the convergence criteria during the transitional phase leading up to complete monetary union. The final phase was to depend on progress achieved by the member states in conforming to the convergence criteria. If these conditions were satisfied, the final stage was scheduled to begin at the end of 1996. With the onset of the currency turmoil of 1992, however, the final stage was re-scheduled to begin on 1 January 1999 by those countries that qualified for membership (Appendix 6A).

The essential "convergence criteria" that were eventually agreed upon were:

1 The national inflation rate not to exceed 1.5 per cent of the best performing member.
2 Budget deficits to be reduced to 3 per cent of GDP and the public debt not to exceed 60 per cent of GDP.
3 The exchange rate to remain within the narrow band of 2.25 per cent for two years before admission to the final stage.
4 Interest rate differentials to be narrowed within 2 per cent of the lowest national rates.

A certain degree of discretion and flexibility was possible in the interpretation of a country's attainment of these targets. In other words, caveats were provided. The fiscal criteria, in particular, were

DOI: 10.1057/9781137371904

subject to a considerable degree of discretion (Article 104c). If the level of a country's primary public debt ratio was declining and approaching the reference value, then the excess was disregarded. Indeed, after the signing of the Maastricht Treaty, only France and Luxembourg had fulfilled these targets on public debt. The re-unification of Germany had caused an inflationary upsurge and a rising fiscal deficit. At the same time, Spain and the UK had joined the EMS in October 1990 within the wider 6 per cent band. From the very outset of the Delors Plan, three major groups of countries could be identified. First there was the original core group under the narrow 2.25 per cent margin of exchange rate fluctuation, which had exhibited the lowest rates of inflation. The second group comprised the high inflation/high public debt countries of Italy, the UK, Spain and Ireland, which had adopted the 6 per cent band of the ERM. Finally, there was the third group of less industrialised countries of Greece and Portugal that remained outside the ERM. Given this extreme divergence in economic attributes between individual countries, a "two-speed" Europe evolved with the northern industrial core countries of Germany, the Netherlands, France and the former EFTA countries, on the one hand, and the high inflation/deficit countries of Spain, Portugal, Ireland, Greece and Italy, on the other hand. In institutional terms, the emergence of a "two speed" Europe was embodied in Article 109J (paragraph 4), which stated that the final stage of EMU would begin by 1 January 1999 regardless of whether the majority of member states conformed with the convergence criteria.

The Maastricht Treaty proposed that the ECB was to be governed by two fundamental principles. First, the Statutes of the ECB declared price stability as its overriding objective (Article 103 of the Treaty and Article 2 of the ECB Charter). Second, the ECB Charter was to be inscribed with political and institutional independence. Doubtless these protocols exhibited a striking resemblance with the Charter of the Bundesbank. This was also reflected in the structure and organisation of the ECB insofar as both had independent Councils formulating the general parameters of monetary policy, which were discharged by their respective Boards. The ECB Council was also given the power to define the ECU central rates within the ERM, the conduct of open market operations and a common exchange rate policy in the event of monetary union. In order to perform these functions, the ECB was provided with funds from the national central banks (Articles 28 and 29) and endowed

DOI: 10.1057/9781137371904

with the ability to accumulate foreign exchange reserves. Consequently, the bank could earn income from its accumulated assets and distribute the revenue to the national central banks according to their respective capital shares (Article 32). This latter provision was intended to ensure that the ECB was to preserve its independent status.

The powers of the European System of Central Banks were considerable and its Governing Council and Executive Board were to discharge these powers (Articles 10 and 11 of the ECB/ESCB Protocol) on the basis of a simple and qualified majority vote. The ESCB was essentially a forum for inter-central bank co-ordination. In the absence of veto powers to members appointed by national central banks, the scope for inter-state conflict was substantial in which the balance of voting power rested with the national central bank governors. Since not all the EU states have joined the euro, the ESCB could not be used as the monetary authority of the eurozone. Its role was therefore purely advisory (Dyson and Featherstone, 1999).

There was still considerable ambiguity over responsibility for the conduct of monetary policy. The Maastricht Treaty divided responsibility for exchange rate policy between the ECB and the EU Economics and Finance Council, which comprised the Cabinet Ministers of member states. Whereas ECOFIN was assigned the role of determining the long-term exchange rate, the ECB presided over short-term interest rate policy and nominal, discretionary changes in the euro exchange rate. Similarly, the ECB was governed by a Board of six members headed by the President but monetary policy was also determined in concert with the Central Bank Governors of the member states. Quite clearly, there was considerable potential for conflict over monetary policy as member countries pursued contradictory national aims.[1] The "unholy trinity" hypothesis stated that in the context of high capital mobility, member states were compelled to choose between monetary autonomy and exchange rate stability. With the abolition of capital controls under the Maastricht Treaty, the maintenance of fixed exchange rates became impossible without closely co-ordinated monetary policies or the introduction of a single currency (Henning Randall, 1998, p.539).

> The posture of the ECB will be particularly important on decision-making within the monetary union because it is granted the right (and obligation) to participate in exchange rate policy making by Article 109 of the Maastricht Treaty. The ECB has the right to be consulted in all exchange rate decisions made by the Council of Ministers. In cases of formal exchange rate regimes,

DOI: 10.1057/9781137371904

> that consultation should endeavour to reach a consensus consistent with the objective of price stability.... In formulating "general orientations" for exchange rate policy, the Council will be able to act on a qualified majority vote. Formal agreements that peg the euro to the dollar or the yen, however, will require a unanimous vote within the Council after consulting not only the ECB but with the European Commission and Parliament as well. (Henning Randall, 1996, p.93)

After the final stage of monetary union, the ECB was given the authority to issue a single currency. The euro was to compete against the US dollar and the Japanese yen as an international vehicular currency. According to Emerson, the direct benefits of a single currency were estimated to account for about 0.05 per cent of the Community GDP when translated into net savings in intra-EC transaction costs and was estimated to accrue one-time seigniorage gains of about $US35bn (Emerson, 1992, p.25). The real benefits, however, were difficult to quantify and were to be realised in the form of greater insulation from the adverse impact of US dollar volatility on the terms of trade. From a political standpoint, it was envisaged that EMU would provide a more coherent and unified voice in international fora and simplify the process of international macroeconomic co-ordination. A common monetary and exchange rate policy, it was assumed, would therefore elevate the political and trade profile of the EU and contribute to a more stable multi-polar world monetary system. But in order to challenge US dollar supremacy, the euro required a sovereign political entity to support its role as international means of payments and reserve asset.

The euro/dollar exchange rate has played an important role in the competitive struggle over markets and investment outlets. Germany, in particular, has been quite vulnerable to fluctuations in the euro/dollar exchange rate as a result of its over-reliance on an export-led strategy of growth. After reaching purchasing power parity (PPP) with the US dollar at the end of 2003, the euro appreciated quite sharply after 2005 to peak at 1.60 dollars in late 2008. The euro stabilised at about 1.45 US dollars over the next three years, which was still well above PPP. The appreciation of the euro during this period has led to a loss of international competitiveness and created considerable instability between the surplus and deficit countries of the eurozone. In order to compensate for this loss of international competitiveness, Germany intensified its policies of wage repression and disinflation.

DOI: 10.1057/9781137371904

Competitive disinflation

Possibly the most contentious and politically sensitive aspect of the Maastricht accord was the technical prohibition of the financing of public deficits by the ECB (Article 21.1 of the ECB Statute). These ideological preferences were informed by the monetarist appeal to the doctrine of "sound finance".[2] Moreover, the ECB was also prohibited from acting as a lender of last resort to a member state experiencing a temporary fiscal crisis, although in theory the ECB could conduct open market operations, which might involve the purchase of government debt in secondary bond markets. In order to prevent the monetisation of public debts, national governments were obliged to maintain low public debt–GDP ratios. This provision of the treaty had important implications for the high deficit members of Italy, Spain, Greece and Portugal, all of whom had a higher reliance upon revenue derived through seigniorage. Given the constraints imposed on the level of public debt, the scope for fiscal expansion to promote employment was severely limited. In fact, the whole paradigm that informed the Delors Plan appeared to be governed by prevailing neoliberal economic doctrines, which relied upon private financial markets to "discipline" so-called profligate governments. The abolition of capital controls also had quite profound implications for the high deficit countries. Capital market liberalisation implied a loss of public control over national interest rates, which would undermine the ability of ERM countries to maintain exchange rate parities. The choice, therefore, was between the imposition of highly restrictive fiscal policies to compensate for the loss of monetary policy instruments or the acceptance of higher margins of exchange rate movements as a means of external adjustment. If exchange rates were irrevocably fixed, however, the very real likelihood of a speculative capital flight could be provoked. In retrospect, financial market liberalisation became incompatible with the existing regime of fixed exchange rates. Even though the ECB would assume monetary control, the national central banks (NCBs) would continue to perform a supervisory role.

> In the event of a banking crisis, these two roles overlap: the national bank, acting as the lender of last resort, would wish to inject liquidity into the financial system; however, it would be constrained given that money supply falls under the remit of the ECB. (Arestis et al., 2001, p.125)

DOI: 10.1057/9781137371904

These glaring contradictions were to emerge during the exchange rate crises of 1992–93. German re-unification had induced a rise in domestic interest rates and the appreciation of the German mark. As the DM appreciated, pressure mounted on the British pound and the Italian lira, which culminated in their withdrawal in scenes reminiscent of the earlier "snake" debacle. Market perceptions about the inability of the high inflation/deficit countries to maintain their respective nominal exchange rates in the event of capital market liberalisation triggered the speculative attack. A series of devaluations was inevitable either because of the self-fulfilling speculative propensities generated by large capital outflows, or by the exhaustion of foreign exchange reserves required to defend the exchange rate.

The exchange rate crises of mid-1992 were accompanied by the political uncertainty surrounding the ratification of the Maastricht Treaty. In early June, the Danish referendum had rejected the Treaty, while the French referendum held in September had generated considerable uncertainty before it was ratified by a small majority. Despite concerted central bank interventions, the Italian lira and British pound continued to attract speculative attacks. Italy's high level of public debt and budget deficit were perceived by the markets to be unsustainable despite the imposition of high real interest rates. Similarly, Britain's high current account deficit and the onset of recession also contributed to the exchange rate crisis as financial markets anticipated a devaluation. By the end of September, British and Italian memberships of the ERM were suspended. The successful ratification of the Maastricht Treaty in France and strong German support for the French exchange rate had the effect of dampening these speculative forces. In the course of the speculative crisis, the Italian lira and the British pound had experienced a nominal, effective depreciation of 16 per cent and 15 per cent respectively. The French franc and German mark remained relatively unchanged within the ERM (Blanden-Hovell, 1994, p.342). Over the next year, however, most of the ERM currencies with the exception of the German mark, Dutch guilder and Irish pound, had fallen below their respective divergence threshold, which culminated in an increase in the permitted band of exchange rate movement to 15 per cent either side of parity within the ERM in August 1993.

The reverberations of the speculative turmoil of 1992–93 postponed the EMU timetable for the final stage. With the continued existence of high public debts, similar speculative attacks were provoked in the absence of

DOI: 10.1057/9781137371904

capital controls. If a country incurred a large stock of public debt and was faced with an impending fiscal crisis because of its inability to refinance the debt, its creditworthiness would come under scrutiny by investors and creditors. Financial markets might perceive the reluctance by the authorities to increase interest rates in order to defend the exchange rate because of the adverse effect this would have on the ability of the government to service the debt. The removal of capital controls and the liberalisation of capital markets within a regime of fixed exchange rates therefore incurred quite considerable risks for high inflation/deficit countries as the debacle of 1992–93 had already demonstrated.

The fiscal constraint imposed by the Maastricht Treaty failed to be entirely convincing. Countries that experienced specific exogenous shocks that temporarily undermined their external balance could not resort to fiscal stabilisation measures or the imposition of capital controls. They would experience a more painful adjustment with the enactment of a restrictive monetary and fiscal programme. The erosion in the efficacy of national fiscal policies imparted a deflationary bias unless fiscal transfers were augmented on the Community level. However, in its existing form, the Community budget was inadequate to perform this function. At the same time, the "one-size-fits-all" monetary policy set by the incumbent European Central Bank restricted the ability of national governments to pursue traditional Keynesian counter-cyclical policies.

In this sense, the fiscal criteria of the Delors Plan were difficult to justify on conventional Keynesian grounds unless there was a corresponding fiscal regime on the supranational level. In the course of the Council of Ministers meeting in Dublin in December 1996, the French proposal that growth as well as price stability should be enshrined as an objective of EMU monetary policy was successfully endorsed (Artis and Winkler, 1997, p.1). The meeting established a new Ministerial "stability council" as a political counterweight to the ECB. Similarly, at the European Summit in Amsterdam in June 1997, the newly elected Socialist government of Jospin endorsed an employment chapter to the Maastricht Treaty, which elevated employment as a parallel goal to price stability (Feldstein, 1997).[3] Despite these compromises, the essential design of EMU continued to be governed by the primary objective of price stability. The neoliberal/monetarist theories that informed the ECB simply failed to recognise the critical role of fiscal policy. Indeed, the Stability and Growth Pact merely reinforced this excessive regime of austerity by enshrining the very strict

DOI: 10.1057/9781137371904

fiscal criteria, which were to be imposed on the member states in the final stage of EMU.

In order to qualify for the final phase of monetary union, each country was therefore impelled to impose highly restrictive macroeconomic policy regimes. There inevitably developed a powerful disinflationary tendency within the Community, which culminated in the process of "competitive disinflation" as each country attempted to pursue a strategy to improve their export competitiveness through lower inflation and lower nominal wages in relation to their competitors. In order to escape from this straightjacket of competitive disinflation, the co-ordination of national fiscal policies was required. This would promote the recycling of surpluses from the structural core regions to the peripheral deficit regions. Since the EC budget could not perform this redistributive function adequately, given its negligible resources, the whole process of economic integration was highly dependent upon the ability and willingness of national governments to co-ordinate their respective fiscal policies. Furthermore, the enormous instability generated by speculative capital flows as a result of deregulated financial markets continued to destabilise the fixed exchange rate regime.

Despite the imposition of quite harsh monetary and fiscal policies, all of the 15 member countries, with the exception of Greece, qualified for membership of the final phase of EMU. The fiscal contraction in Italy was quite harsh. From a budget deficit of 10 per cent of GDP in 1993, Italy reduced the ratio to 2.5 per cent when the European Summit met in London in early May to finalise membership of the eurozone. In Italy, this fiscal target was achieved through a severe curtailment of government expenditure and the imposition of a one-off "Eurotax", which raised about $US3 billion. On the eve of the single currency, both Belgium and Italy with 118.1 per cent and Greece with 107.7 per cent failed to meet their respective public debt–GDP ratios of 60 per cent, while for the budget deficit criteria, all of the 15 countries achieved the target of 3 per cent of GDP.[4] Indeed, the combined EU budget deficit fell from 6.1 per cent of Combined EU GDP in 1993 to 2.7 per cent in 1997. Table 6.1 summarises the performance of each country in relation to the fiscal criteria in March 1998.

The problem of fiscal solidarity between the member states was never fully resolved. For instance, if a member state withdraws from the EMU and resorts to debt monetisation in order to finance its fiscal deficit, this action could provoke a "bandwagon" effect by other deficit

DOI: 10.1057/9781137371904

TABLE 6.1 *The Maastricht criteria on public debt and budget deficits (March 1998)*

Maastricht criteria	Debt as a % of GDP (60%)	Budget deficit as a % of GDP (3%)
Austria	64.7	2.3
Belgium	118.1	1.3
Britain	53.0	0.6
Denmark	59.5	−1.1
Finland	53.6	−0.3
France	58.1	2.9
Germany	61.2	2.5
Greece	107.7	2.2
Ireland	59.5	−1.1
Italy	118.1	2.5
Luxembourg	7.1	−1.0
Netherlands	70.0	1.6
Portugal	60.0	2.2
Spain	67.4	2.2
Sweden	74.1	−0.5

Source: European Commission, 1998.

countries. As a result, financial stress in one country could raise doubts about the degree of financial solidarity across the Community and affect the financial credibility of government bonds. Similarly, inflationary differentials between member states could translate into diverging real effective exchange rates (REER) and provoke capital flights from the high to the low inflation member states. Since the official interest rate was set by the ECB across the eurozone, the high inflation member states would experience lower real interest rates, which could induce excessive credit creation and generate speculative asset price booms. With the liberalisation of capital markets these negative "spill-over" effects could provoke quite destructive and self-fulfilling speculative flows of capital in the absence of a coherent regulatory framework on the supranational level. Quite apart from fiscal co-ordination, the Maastricht accord relied almost exclusively on the efficacy of the financial markets to discipline "profligate" governments. For the deficit countries, however, the prolongation of disinflationary policies would prove to be counter-productive as the sovereign debt crises of 2009–12 were to reveal quite starkly. The imposition of high interest rates could cause the external debt to deteriorate even further through a cumulative increase in their respective debt servicing ratios. In the most indebted countries of Italy, Greece, Belgium, Portugal, Ireland and Spain, interest

DOI: 10.1057/9781137371904

TABLE 6.2 *The Maastricht targets for inflation and interest rates (April 1998)*

Maastricht criteria	Inflation* (%) Target (3.2%)		Long-term interest rates# Target (7.7%)
	1997	1998	1998
Austria	1.1	1.5	5.6
Belgium	1.4	1.3	5.7
Britain	1.8	2.3	7.0
Denmark	1.9	2.1	6.2
Finland	1.3	2.0	5.9
France	1.2	1.0	5.5
Germany	1.4	1.7	5.6
Greece	5.2	4.5	9.8
Ireland	1.2	3.3	6.2
Italy	1.8	2.1	6.7
Luxembourg	1.4	1.6	5.6
Netherlands	1.8	2.3	5.5
Portugal	1.8	2.2	6.2
Spain	1.8	2.2	6.3
Sweden	1.9	1.5	6.5

Note: * Within 1.5% average of the lowest three. # Within 2% average of inflation's lowest three.
Source: European Commission, 1988.

payments on their public debt had accounted for over 10 per cent of their respective GDPs and represented more than 20 per cent of their respective government expenditure in 1991 (Emerson, 1992, p.123). Table 6.2 summarises the Maastricht criteria on long-term interest rates and inflation in April 1998.

With the curtailment of fiscal policies and the eventual abolition of exchange rate policies on the national level, a corresponding regulatory regime was required for the Community as a whole. The other alternative would involve closer macroeconomic co-ordination between member states. In the latter case, it was difficult to envisage the willingness of surplus countries to finance the deficit countries. Fiscal federalism would appear to be the logical corollary of monetary union. The Community budget would perform the redistributive and stabilisation functions previously the exclusive domain of national governments. This necessarily implied a form of political federation and an expansion in the legislative and budgetary powers of the European parliament. In such a scenario, the EU budget would acquire the critical functions of fiscal stabilisation and redistribution. Given the size and structure of the Community budget – the automatic stabilisers required to act as "shock absorbers" to

DOI: 10.1057/9781137371904

cushion the effects of asymmetrical regional shocks in the event of monetary union – continued to be inadequate (Giovannini and Spaventa, 1991, p.101). This was in stark contrast to the US system of federalism in which automatic fiscal transfers on the national level tended to finance regional fiscal imbalances. According to the MacDougall Report of 1977, the size of EU budget would need to increase from its existing 1.5 per cent of combined EU GDP to at least 7.5 per cent of the Community GDP in order to perform this stabilising role (Arestis and Sawyer, 2006a, p.19). It was precisely this deeply flawed institutional design of the euro which could threaten its future survival. As Gilpin argues:

> Because Euro-zone members are not allowed to use independent monetary policies and pull themselves out of a shock-induced recession, they would normally utilize such a fiscal policy as tax cuts or public works to stimulate demand. The EU itself could have a fiscal policy to distribute financial resources to a depressed area to stimulate demand. However, the role of fiscal policy in Euroland has not been determined. Although it is unclear whether or not members will retain some fiscal powers, the Stability Pact demanded by Germany suggests those members' fiscal powers will be greatly restricted. (2000, p.208)

Conclusion

Competitive disinflation or "beggar-thy-neighbour" deflation became a substitute for competitive devaluations as member countries pursued a strategy to improve their export competitiveness in terms of lower inflation. Whereas competitive devaluations generated inflationary tendencies, competitive disinflation functioned in the opposite direction by producing a cumulative process of deflation (Fitoussi, 1993). The discipline imposed by the ERM in which Germany acted as the nominal exchange rate anchor, imparted powerful disinflationary impulses throughout the EMS zone. Competitive disinflation was deceptively simple. One country's exports represented another country's imports. This implied that cumulative deflation caused by each country's pursuit of lower inflation in order to accumulate a trade surplus also led to the curtailment of imports by dampening the level of domestic demand. This process of cumulative disinflation has contributed to the stagnation of the European economy since the 1990s. The broad outlines of this slump syndrome were evident by the severe curtailment of effective demand within the Community. The ultimate economic consequences

DOI: 10.1057/9781137371904

of competitive disinflation were evident in rising unemployment and a decline in productive investment. As tax revenues fell as a result the onset of economic stagnation, each government was confronted by fiscal retrenchment. Since the ability to resort to foreign borrowings was constrained by the Maastricht Treaty and by the penalties imposed by deregulated financial markets, there was an overwhelming trend toward public sector expenditure cut-backs and the privatisation of public assets in order to balance the national budget. Taken as a whole, these policies constituted a radical dismantling of the post-war "social market" regime of accumulation and the winding back of traditional Keynesian countercyclical policies to maintain full employment.

From the standpoint of public policy, the central dilemma posed by monetary union was the problem of country-specific and asymmetrical shocks. In short, how would governments cope with business cycle stabilisation if the scope for fiscal policy was limited by the exchange rate constraint? In short, the Maastricht Treaty's strict fiscal criteria had severely limited the scope for national governments to pursue countercyclical policies. At the same time, the absence of independent monetary and exchange rate policy instruments made it impossible for member states to monetise their public debts since the national debt was now denominated in the euro. Even though endogenous, country-specific shocks continued to occur after monetary union, national governments were obliged to surrender a considerable degree of autonomy in their ability to pursue the macroeconomic objectives of full employment. If fiscal co-ordination proved to be inadequate, then the other means by which to enact stabilisation policies was through a Community budget. This necessarily implied fiscal federalism. Unfortunately, the Community budget lacked the critical mass and the political capacity to perform this crucial role.

DOI: 10.1057/9781137371904

Appendix 6A: Major features of the three EMU stages

Economic	Monetary
Stage 1	
▸ Completion of the internal market ▸ Strengthened competition policy ▸ Full implementation of the reform of the structural funds. ▸ Enhanced co-ordination and surveillance. ▸ Budgetary adjustment in the high debt/deficit countries	▸ Capital market liberalisation ▸ Enhanced monetary and exchange rate co-ordination. ▸ Re-alignments possible but infrequent. ▸ All EC countries in the narrow band ERM. ▸ Extended use of the ECU.
Stage 2	
▸ Evolution and adoption of stage 1 policies. ▸ Review of macroeconomic adjustments.	▸ Establishment of the Eurofed ▸ Possible narrowing of EMS bands.
Stage 3	
▸ Definitive budgetary co-ordination system. ▸ Possible strengthening of structural and regional policies.	▸ Eurofed in charge of monetary policy. ▸ Irrevocably fixed exchange rates. ▸ Introduction of the euro.

Source: Emerson, 1992, p.40.

Appendix 6B: Euro membership, 2002–12

In 2002 the euro replaced the national currencies of 12 countries: Austria, Belgium, Finland, France, Germany, Greece, Ireland, Italy, Luxembourg, Netherlands, Portugal and Spain. Denmark, Sweden and the UK chose not to join the eurozone. In May 2004, 10 new member states gained membership of the EU: Czech Republic, Estonia, Hungary, Latvia, Lithuania, Poland, Slovenia, Slovakia, Cyprus and Malta. In 2007, Bulgaria and Romania also joined the EU. Five of these new member states have joined the eurozone: Slovenia (2007), Cyprus and Malta (2008), Slovakia (2009) and Estonia (2011).

Notes

1 These tensions surfaced over the appointment of the first ECB President. While the Germans supported the appointment of Win Duisenberg – the Dutch central banker and head of the EMI – for the first eight-year term, the French nominated their own candidate, Jean-Claude Trichet, the Governor of the Bank of France. The final compromise witnessed the appointment of Duisenberg for the first four years and Trichet for the second four years.

2 As was predicted by Kalecki as early as 1943, opposition to full employment emerged as a result of the restoration of the class power of business and rentier interests. This hegemonic transition from the post-war Keynesian consensus was informed by the abandonment of full employment and the elevation of price stability as the overriding aim of macroeconomic policy. According to Kalecki, these ideological objections to the maintenance of full employment were: "(1) the dislike of government interference on the problem of employment as such; (2) the dislike of the direction of government spending (public investment and subsidising consumption); (3) the dislike of the social and political changes resulting from the *maintenance* of full employment" (1943, p.324). With the onset of stagflation during the 1970s and 1980s as a result of successive oil price shocks, the rise of Monetarism was used as an ideological device to invoke the spectre of inflation in order to oppose wage rises and increase the share of profits in national income. Indeed, the existence of full employment during the post-war boom had deprived the "captains of industry" the weapon of the reserve army of labour to depress the level of wages. Instead, the spectre of inflation was exploited as a means by which to impose the burden of adjustment onto wages and employment. The contention that government intervention would erode "business confidence" was also invoked to oppose social spending and the ideological opposition to government deficit spending on the basis of the doctrine of "sound finance" and the economic dogma of the "crowding out" of private investment. As Kalecki quite presciently declared: "Hence, budget deficits necessary to carry out government intervention must be regarded as perilous. The social function of the doctrine of 'sound finance' is to make the level of employment dependent on the 'state of confidence'" (1943, p.325).

3 This became known as "Maastricht 2". Despite French insistence on promoting employment as a principle objective of the Stability Pact, the general ideological tenor of the Treaty continued to support restrictive policies.

4 Belgium and Italy were able to convince the EU authorities that their primary debt ratios were falling at a sufficient rate in order to qualify for membership.

DOI: 10.1057/9781137371904

7

The European Debt Crisis

Abstract: *A cloud of uncertainty has enveloped the fate of the euro. After three decades in the construction of European Monetary Union, culminating in the birth of the euro in 1999, the whole edifice has been shaken to its very foundations by the recent sovereign debt crises, which have engulfed the peripheral, deficit countries of the eurozone (i.e., Greece, Portugal, Spain and Ireland). These profound asymmetrical shocks, emanating from the global financial crisis of 2007–09, could eventually threaten the internal cohesion of the eurozone. The aim of this chapter is to critically evaluate the efficacy of the neoliberal strategy, which has informed the Maastricht Treaty and how the evolution of the euro project now encounters the limitations and the deleterious legacy of this ill-conceived institutional framework.*

Lucarelli, Bill. *Endgame for the Euro: A Critical History.* Basingtoke: Palgrave Macmillan, 2013.
DOI: 10.1057/9781137371904.

 DOI: 10.1057/9781137371904

Introduction

A cloud of uncertainty has enveloped the fate of the euro. After three decades in the construction of European Monetary Union, culminating in the birth of the euro in 1999, the whole edifice has been shaken to its very foundations by the recent sovereign debt crises, which have engulfed the peripheral, deficit countries of the eurozone (i.e., Greece, Portugal, Spain and Ireland). These profound asymmetrical shocks, emanating from the global financial crisis of 2007–09, could eventually threaten the internal cohesion of the eurozone. In order to understand the structural dynamics of the current crisis, it is necessary to examine the longstanding internal contradictions that the system has inherited from its inception under the Maastricht Treaty of 1992 and the neoliberal strategy, which has governed its evolution. The aim of this chapter is to critically evaluate the efficacy of this neoliberal strategy and how the evolution of the euro project now encounters the limitations and the deleterious legacy of this ill-conceived institutional framework. The original design of the euro and the European Central Bank under the aegis of the Maastricht Treaty in 1992 will be analysed to reveal the fragile foundations upon which the eurozone was constructed. It will be argued that German neo-mercantilism was at the very core of Europe's descent into a seemingly irreversible phase of stagnation. In the absence of fiscal federalism, the sovereign debt crises that have enveloped the peripheral, deficit countries will only worsen, pushing the eurozone into a possible phase of debt-deflation.

Origins of the crisis

Although the financial crisis originated in the US in the wake of the subprime loans debacle, the contagion soon engulfed Europe as a result of the exposure of European banks to mortgage-backed securities and other toxic assets. The after-shocks of the cessation of inter-bank lending in late 2008 triggered the onset of the sovereign debt crisis. The ensuing recession in Europe led to the sudden rise in fiscal deficits as the automatic stabilisers were activated. Indeed, the sharp contraction of the level of effective demand in Europe was more severe than in the US, which could be attributed to the more urgent reaction from the US authorities in the implementation of fiscal and monetary stimulus

DOI: 10.1057/9781137371904

(Onaran, 2010). The peripheral, deficit countries of the eurozone were the most vulnerable to these external shocks in which Greece emerged as the perceived weakest link by the bond markets. As early as September/October 2008, as the international financial crisis reached a critical point, the spreads on Greek government debt began to diverge quite dramatically from the benchmark German government bonds. The general flight to safety in the aftermath of the collapse of Lehman Brothers provoked a sudden contraction of liquidity and a full-scale credit crunch (Galbraith, 2010, p.3).

As early as September 2008, the ECB supported the large Euro banks by injecting liquidity and accepting their toxic assets as collateral for private borrowings, which the banks had accumulated in their exposure to the mortgage-backed securities originated in the US. This allowed the banks to deleverage in a desperate attempt to restore their balance sheets. By 2009, the private banks demanded higher risk premiums in their willingness to lend to the peripheral countries. In this context, the commercial banks sought to increase their liquidity preferences by reducing their holdings of long-term securities, which was accommodated by the ECB (Lapavitsas, *et al.*, 2010, p.7). The ensuing credit crunch, however, only further aggravated and prolonged the economic downturn and led to an avalanche of bankruptcies, which swelled the ranks of the unemployed. The Greek crisis was made even more severe by the asymmetric shocks experienced within the eurozone as the core countries of Germany and France found themselves in deep recession. The de-synchronisation of the business cycle between the weaker deficit countries and the surplus countries of the core regions only served to intensify these asymmetric shocks. It was the reluctance of the German monetary authorities to pursue a reflationary strategy that amplified the crisis in Greece and in the other peripheral countries. Under these circumstances, a common monetary stabilisation strategy by the ECB proved to be counter-productive. More significantly, the imposition of fiscal austerity in the peripheral, deficit countries has made matters worse, pushing these countries to the brink of a deflationary trap (Pelagidis, 2009, p.103).

Inflationary divergences between Germany and the peripheral countries have had a cumulative effect during the first decade of the euro to the extent that these differentials have represented an estimated 20 per cent effective devaluation by Germany in real terms relative to Portugal, Spain, Ireland and Greece (Stockhammer, 2010, p.17). Over the same

DOI: 10.1057/9781137371904

period, the narrowing of interest rate differentials between the member states since the introduction of the euro in 1999 has contributed to the real estate bubbles in Spain, Ireland and Greece. However, it was not until the sovereign debt crisis of 2010 that these inflation differentials were reflected in diverging yields on government bonds between Germany and the peripheral states. At the same time, the current account deficits of the peripheral countries imparted a powerful contractionary impulse on domestic demand in Germany as net exports and private investment fell sharply. The overall effect was a drift toward stagnation and recession. By the second quarter of 2009, the unemployment rate in the European Union had increased by 2.4 per cent from a year earlier to reach 9.4 per cent and continued to rise to 10.9 per cent a year later. The sharpest increases in unemployment were experienced in the peripheral countries of Ireland, Spain, Portugal and Greece. Since the inception of the Maastricht Treaty in 1992 until 2010, total debt (private and public) of the peripheral countries has risen between two and three times (Lapavitsas, *et al.*, 2010, pp.1–2). According to the *BIS Quarterly Review* in June 2010, the eurozone banks had an exposure of $US727bn in Spain, $US244bn in Portugal, $US206bn in Greece and $US402bn in Ireland. The sum total of bank exposure by the end of 2009 in the four countries stood at about $US1574bn, of which $US254bn, or about 16 per cent was government debt. Most of these loans were held by French and German banks (BIS, 2010, pp.18–19).

As the credit crunch spread from Wall Street to the rest of the world, central banks enacted highly expansionary monetary policies. However, the reluctance of the commercial banks to resume lending to member states imparted upward pressure on government bond yields, which merely encouraged speculative attacks on those countries with a high exposure to sovereign debt. The wave of speculation in bond markets in early 2010 was fuelled by an upsurge in the yield spreads for government debt. Panic soon broke out in bond markets as doubts were raised over the ability of some of the peripheral countries – identified with the acronym of the PIIGS (i.e., Portugal, Ireland, Italy, Greece and Spain) – to service their debt obligations. This was reflected in the demands for a higher risk premium on these government bonds. Indeed, the more that these perceived concerns over the possibility of default mounted, the higher the premiums demanded by the bond markets and therefore the greater the debt incurred by these governments (Vaisse, 2009, p.4). The whole process became dangerously self-reinforcing. More importantly,

DOI: 10.1057/9781137371904

however, was the threat that this sovereign debt posed to the large German and French banks. According to the IMF, European banks held a higher proportion of non-performing loans than their counterparts in the US. By the end of 2009, these toxic assets were estimated at over a $US1 trillion in the US after the massive rescue operations by the US Federal Reserve and the US Treasury. By contrast, these toxic assets were estimated at over $US1.4 trillion in Europe, while capital injections by European central banks had been minimal. The magnitude of the sovereign debt crisis therefore threatened to dwarf the financial meltdown in the US.

By the end of 2009, the BIS estimated the exposure of European banks to sovereign debt was equivalent to about two thirds of international exposure to the debts incurred by Greece, Ireland, Portugal and Spain. In April 2010, there was a major stampede out of Greek government bonds, which caused the interest rate on the two-year Greek bonds to surge to as high as 19 per cent. As speculation over the likelihood of default reached fever pitch, the cost of credit default swaps (CDS) for Greek bonds peaked, which led to the downgrading of Greek bonds by international ratings agencies to junk bond status. In early May 2010, the member states finally agreed to establish a €720 billion stabilisation fund for the eurozone government-backed securities (Toporowsky, 2010, p.3). A precedent was set as the European Commission introduced the European Financial Stabilisation Mechanism (EFSM), which injected €110 billion to bail out Greek bonds and mobilised €500bn from member states and an additional €250bn from the IMF[1] to prevent the crisis from spreading to the other peripheral, deficit countries of Europe.[2]

The international financial crisis exposed these mounting imbalances within the eurozone and hastened a new phase in the global recession of 2008–09 (Onaran, 2010, p.23). In stark contrast to the UK and the US, the eurozone countries were slow to act in stimulating their economies and were caught in complete disarray. Burgeoning budget deficits throughout the eurozone were doubtless generated "endogenously" through the sudden collapse in output and investment rather than through government "profligacy". Member states were forced to finance their respective rescue plans by borrowing from financial markets, which, in the context of a severe credit crunch, made these operations more expensive. The commercial banks curtailed their funding to the peripheral countries in the eurozone and demanded exorbitant interest rates to cover escalating risk premiums. Indeed, one of the ultimate ironies was that the very same banks, which had been rescued by the ECB, were now stampeding out of the eurozone into the temporary safe haven of the US bond markets. Furthermore, the expansionary fiscal policies eventually enacted by the eurozone member states provided a temporary respite for these commercial banks. But as tax revenues collapsed as a result of the recession, member states, most notably in the peripheral regions, experienced a sovereign debt crisis. Yet again, it was the very same banks, supported by the IMF and the EU Commission that demanded a program of austerity and wage cuts and threatened to curtail their lending to those governments that failed to comply.

The fact that the ECB was willing to purchase government bonds in the secondary bond markets rather than directly suggests that the original "no bail out" of insolvent governments was temporarily suspended. This glaring dichotomy only served to further highlight the flawed architecture of the Maastricht Treaty. In the absence of a common fiscal regime, analogous to the US Treasury, the European banking system was exposed to the risk of defaults by sovereign states. The potential "moral hazard" risks invoked by this scenario, compelled the ECB to incur the ultimate risks by purchasing these bonds in the secondary bond markets (Whelan, 2010, p.10). In other words, the ECB was acting as "market maker" of last resort. This allowed the banking system to restore their balance sheets and increase their liquidity, even though renewed lending would not be assured in the event of the onset of a liquidity trap. The ultimate political and social costs, however, were incurred by the peripheral deficit countries, which were forced to impose quite severe austerity measures in order to placate the private commercial banks.

The legacy of the Maastricht treaty

In order to grasp the dynamics of the current crisis, it is necessary to understand the historical context and the institutional framework, which have defined the broad contours of Europe's descent into a state of semi-permanent economic stagnation. Europe's protracted structural crisis has been the direct legacy of over three decades of neoliberal policies of disinflation, which have informed its evolution toward monetary union, enshrined in the strict "convergence criteria" of the Maastricht Treaty and reinforced by the Stability and Growth Pact of 1997. The peculiar institutional characteristics of the European Central Bank and Germany's

DOI: 10.1057/9781137371904

incessant neo-mercantilist pursuit of competitive disinflation within the eurozone have created the conditions for this self-reinforcing and seemingly irreversible process of cumulative decline and stagnation. Despite the various attempts to encourage regional convergence, the neoliberal strategy of "negative integration" has only exacerbated these regional disparities and income inequalities within the eurozone. The current crisis is to a large extent the culmination of this longstanding and deep-seated phase of stagnation within the eurozone over the past 20 years.

In 1992, the Maastricht Treaty established the basic architecture for EMU and the institutional design of the European Central Bank, which was essentially modelled on the Bundesbank (Lucarelli, 2004a). In the absence of political union, the eventual birth of the euro in 1999 created a central bank that was entirely devoid of a corresponding fiscal framework or the existence of a common European Treasury, analogous to the US Treasury. At the same time, a quite narrow and arbitrary set of fiscal criteria were enshrined by the Maastricht Treaty, which have since imparted a powerful disinflationary impulse throughout the eurozone. This fiscal straightjacket has been responsible to a large extent for Europe's prolonged phase of stagnation and high levels of unemployment. As has been argued in earlier chapters, one of the major reasons for this phase of stagnation can be attributed to German ideological preferences for competitive disinflation in order to maintain their export competitiveness (Lucarelli, 2011–12). Consequently, as soon as exchange rates were irrevocably locked into the Exchange Rate Mechanism, the peripheral deficit countries were no longer able to restore their respective international competitiveness through exchange rate devaluations. This deflationary dynamic resembled the disastrous experience of the gold standard regime during the inter-war years. The surrender of monetary and exchange rate policies to the ECB has compelled the deficit countries to adjust internally through a programme of severe austerity. The absence of a common eurozone exchange rate policy and central bank open market operations implied that the exchange rate of the euro was determined almost entirely by international futures and derivatives markets. The sole means of adjustment was now imposed on the level of prices and nominal wages.

In a rather inexplicable violation of the basic principles of central banking, the Maastricht Treaty's design of the European Central Bank designated that the "lender of last resort" function should be prohibited (Article 21.1 of the ECB Statute).[3] In other words, the ECB was prevented from rescuing member states in the event of a sovereign debt crisis.[4]

DOI: 10.1057/9781137371904

Similarly, the decentralised Euro-system of central banks has created a dangerous vacuum in terms of the supervisory role of pan-European banks. The constraints imposed on the ECB by the Maastricht Treaty has made it almost impossible for the ECB to implement a coherent and uniform set of monetary policies because of the continued existence of inflationary differentials across the eurozone. At the same time, the excessive growth of aggregate demand in the peripheral countries, in the years preceding the outbreak of the global financial crisis, had contributed to the deterioration of their respective current account deficits. These intra-eurozone current account imbalances are highlighted in Figures 7.1 and 7.2. The imposition of a "one-size-fits-all" monetary policy by the ECB has only exacerbated these asymmetrical relations between the low inflation and high inflation countries. With the official interest rate set by the ECB over the entire eurozone, the monetary transmission mechanism has led to the high inflation countries experiencing a relatively low real rate of interest, which has induced asset price booms, most notably in real estate in the deficit countries of Ireland, Spain, Portugal and Greece (Krugman, 2011). The divergences of real effective exchange rates caused by these inflationary differentials are reflected in Figure 7.3.

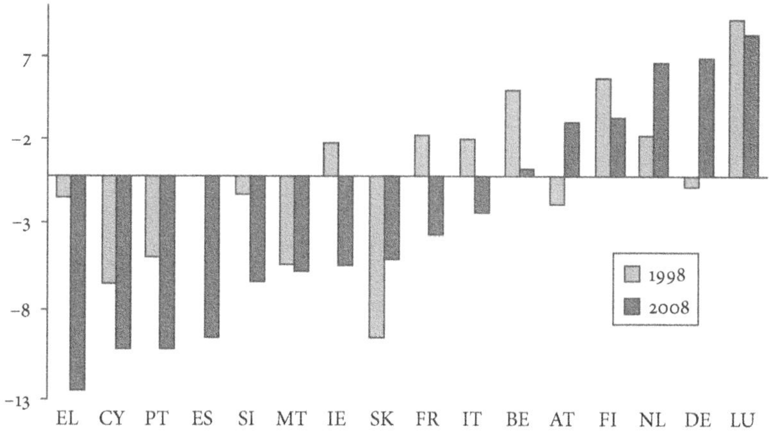

FIGURE 7.1 *Current account positions, eurozone member states (% of GDP, 1998–2008)*

Note: Abbreviations: EL = Estonia; CY = Cyprus; PT = Portugal; ES = Spain; SI = Slovenia; MT = Malta; IE = Ireland; SK = Slovakia; FR = France; IT = Italy BE = Belgium; AT = Austria; FI = Finland; NL = Netherlands; DE= Germany; LU = Luxembourg.

Source: http://ec.europa.eu/economy_finance/publications/publication14650_en.pdf

DOI: 10.1057/9781137371904

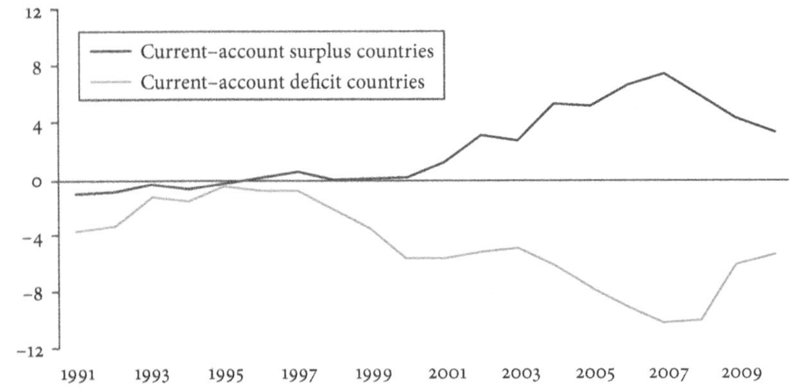

FIGURE 7.2 *Current account positions, eurozone surplus and deficit countries (1991–2010, as % of GDP)*

Source: http://ec.europa.eu/economy_finance/publications/qr_euro_area/2010/pdf/qrea201001en.pdf.

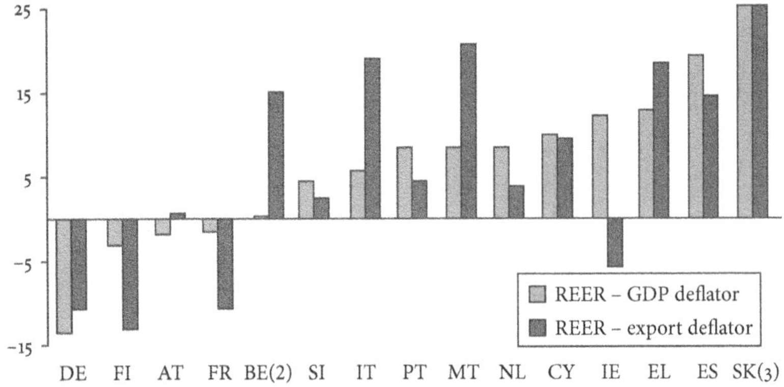

FIGURE 7.3 *Changes in real effective exchange rates (intra and total), eurozone member states (%, 1998 to 2008)*

Source: http://ec.europa.eu/economy_finance/publications/publication14650_en.pdf.

In short, the EMU was devoid of any mechanism that allowed the member states to monetise their fiscal deficits. Furthermore, the real power to issue banknotes in the refinancing operations of the commercial banks resided in the Council of the Euro-system. According to Spethmann and Steiger: "The Council does not only determine the refinancing rate, which is equal to all NCBs, and the amount of liquidity to be allocated in the Euroystem, but the distribution of central bank money to the different NCBs is also determined by their share in the ECB's capital" (Spethmann and Steiger, 2004, p.56). Membership of the EMU has deprived the national central banks of the ability to purchase government bonds in exchange for base money. As a result, the privileges of seigniorage traditionally enjoyed by sovereign states by virtue of their monopoly over the issuing of fiat money was effectively surrendered to the ECB. This implied the very real possibility of national governments defaulting on their sovereign debt in the event of a major financial crisis. Since the sovereign debt was no longer denominated in the national currency or state money, but was now denominated in euros, national governments have not only surrendered their privileges of seigniorage, but also of the ability to monetise their deficits. Under these circumstances, the ECB could ultimately decide whether it would accept national government debt and the terms by which it would do so (Arestis and Sawyer, 2010b, p.9). According to Papadimitriou *et al.*:

> When a private entity goes into debt, its liabilities are another entity's assets: there is no net financial asset creation. When a sovereign government issues debt, it creates an asset for the private sector without an offsetting private sector liability. Hence government issuance of debt results in net financial asset creation for the private sector. Private debt is *debt*, but government debt is *financial wealth* for the private sector. A build-up of private debt should raise concerns, because the private sector cannot run persistent deficits. However, a sovereign government, as the monopoly issuer of its own currency, can always make payments on its debt by crediting bank accounts; those interest payments are non-government income, while the debt is non-government assets. (2010, p.11, emphasis in original)

In the absence of a corresponding fiscal regime on the supranational level, the eurozone has experienced a prolonged period of disinflation and persistently high rates of unemployment. Since the ECB could not directly supply money to the commercial banks (quantitative easing), this deflationary impetus becomes more pervasive. In the eurozone, the member states have irrevocably surrendered their monopoly of issuing fiat money and by so doing have lost their ability to monetise their fiscal deficits (Arestis and Sawyer, 2010a, p.3). Moreover, the imposition of the SGP imposed quite severe limits on fiscal deficits by national governments. At present, the EU budget – estimated at only 1.5 per cent of the combined EU GDP – simply cannot perform the functions of stabilisation

DOI: 10.1057/9781137371904

and redistribution within the EU. The inability of the ECB to monetise public debt has therefore constrained national governments to deploy expansionary fiscal policy in order to mitigate the deleterious effects of recession (Palley, 2010, p.1). The Stability and Growth Pact has had the overall effect of curtailing the efficacy of automatic stabilisation.[5]

Conversely, if governments were able to borrow in their own national currencies, the prospect of default would be very remote, if not impossible. Indeed, the entire rationale for the very existence of central banks rests on their ability to refinance and manage government debt through the principles of functional finance. This critical function was effectively abolished under the rules designed by the Maastricht Treaty. The neoliberal assumption that commercial banks and their inter-bank markets were more efficient at evaluating financial risks than central banks informed the original design of the Maastricht Treaty (Toporowsky, 2010, p.3). These neoliberal nostrums were inextricably linked to the logic of financialisation. Budget deficits were therefore no longer financed according to the tenets of functional finance, but held and reinvested in short-term financial assets in the form of bonds and other types of interest-bearing capital (Frangakis and Huffschmid, 2006, p.39). The surrender of monetary sovereignty by national governments thus imposed unnecessary financial constraints since they were now impelled to borrow from capital markets in order to finance their deficits. This fiscal constraint has made national governments captive to the dictates of financial markets in the formulation of national policy.

Consequently, under the existing neoliberal regime of EMU, the tenets of functional financing in relation to fiscal policy no longer applied.[6] In the absence of a supranational Treasury, analogous to the US system of governance, the Euro-system was devoid of any *direct* mechanisms by which to monetise their fiscal deficits.[7] This implied that each member state was deprived of the conventional Keynesian instruments of fiscal activism to maintain high levels of employment, especially in the event of a recession or an adverse asymmetrical shock. The Greek crisis exposed one of the major institutional weaknesses of the existing Maastricht regime – the lack of a corresponding fiscal framework on the supranational level to mitigate the effects of recession and stagnation and the capacity to act as a counter-cyclical mechanism in stabilising these powerful asymmetrical shocks. Even though the ECB acted as a lender of last resort to the European commercial banks, it could not, under its existing Charter, play the same role in relation to its own member states. Unlike

DOI: 10.1057/9781137371904

most central banks, the ECB was prohibited from directly purchasing government bonds of the member states. These limitations proved to be quite disastrous as the sovereign debt crisis threatened to spread to the other peripheral deficit countries. For the weaker, deficit countries, the choice becomes quite stark: either they default and increase the likelihood of breaking away from the eurozone, or they are compelled to adjust internally through the imposition of a severe program of austerity. Quite clearly, the institutional flaws inherited by the Maastricht regime and informed by monetarist/neoliberal economic doctrines, now act as a serious obstacle to a synchronised recovery of the eurozone.

German neo-mercantilism

Germany's pursuit of neo-mercantilist austerity can be described by applying the Kaleckian theory of foreign trade. In his short but succinct essay, *On Foreign Trade and Domestic Exports*, Kalecki (1969) develops an elegant analysis of this neo-mercantilist logic. He introduces the concept of aggregate profits, which are equal to business consumption, *plus* investment *plus* the balance of foreign trade. In order to stimulate investment through an increase in domestic net profits, the balance of trade component of profits must increase. In other words, a trade surplus must be achieved. Kalecki makes a crucial distinction between an increase in the export surplus (exports minus imports) and absolute exports. An increase in exports would lead, *ceteris paribus*, to a rise in the surplus of foreign trade but would also induce an increase in demand for imports, most notably in raw materials and intermediate goods required for an expansion in production.

The increase in the balance of trade is denoted by s and the corresponding increase in imports and exports by i and e respectively:

$$e = i + s \tag{1}$$

Consequently only a proportion of the total increase in exports contributes to the increase in the balance of trade and thus to aggregate profits. The remainder is used for additional imports necessary for higher levels of output. If the relative share of profits in the aggregate value of production is denoted by the symbol β, production will increase by s/β. Moreover, if the ratio of imports to the value of aggregate production is denoted as α, then the increase in imports will be:

DOI: 10.1057/9781137371904

$$i = \beta(s/\alpha) \quad (2)$$

Thus we obtain:

$$s/i = e - i/i = \alpha/\beta \quad (3)$$

The ratio between the trade balance and net exports is the same as that between the relative share of profits in the value of aggregate production. In the period of expansion of investment, aggregate profits increased because of the rise in the item "investment" by k, but fell by s as a result of the decline in the item "balance of trade". As a general rule, the increased profits amounted to $k - s$. Thus, if one denotes β as the relative share of profits in the value of aggregate production and the ratio of imports to this value as α, the increase in the value of production corresponding to the increase in profits by $k - s$ is equal to $(k - s)/\alpha$ and the corresponding rise in imports to $[(k - s)/\alpha]\beta$.

It follows directly that:

$$k = s(1 + \alpha/\beta) \quad (4)$$

"It is now clear what are the advantages of an upswing stimulated by means of securing a surplus in foreign trade" (Kalecki, 1969, p.25).

This mercantilist logic was further reinforced by Germany's insistence that it also pursue disinflationary policies domestically, thereby setting in train a deflationary spiral throughout the eurozone.[8] By doing so, the German authorities were enacting policies which depressed the level of effective demand in the eurozone and therefore had a negative effect on their own exports.[9] Indeed, the unwillingness of the surplus countries to provide an expansionary impetus in order to expand employment and aggregate demand appeared to be ultimately self-defeating. The supreme irony was that while Germany accused the deficit countries of profligacy and "living beyond their means" it also relied upon these very same countries to generate demand for its industrial exports, which tended to be highly income-elastic. It is difficult to envisage how the weaker deficit countries would restore their export competitiveness in the absence of an exchange rate devaluation which was, of course, ruled out under the euro. These policies have doubtless depressed the level of effective demand throughout the eurozone, but unlike German neo-mercantilism, the countries of the eurozone have not been able to generate sufficient external demand to compensate for their loss of domestic markets. The end result witnessed a phase of debilitating deflation induced by policies of

DOI: 10.1057/9781137371904

wage repression and rising unemployment (Soros, 2010, p.2). By imposing domestic austerity and wage repression, foreign firms were restricted from penetrating the German market. Competitive disinflation, in turn, improved Germany's export competitiveness and compelled domestic firms to seek external markets as a result of the lack of effective demand in the domestic market.

At the same time, the accumulation of German export surpluses generated the export of capital, either directly through an increase in the share of aggregate profits, or indirectly through the beneficial effects that were imparted by virtue of the fact that as a surplus country, Germany acquired the status of an international financial centre. Domestic firms were thus able to access credit domestically at more favorable terms. Within Germany, the close linkages between the major banks and the leading industrial conglomerates, tended to reinforce this neo-mercantilist logic (Halevi and Kriesler, 2004, p.34). Ultimately, the burden of adjustment was borne by the European working class in terms of high unemployment and fiscal austerity (Carchedi, 2001, p.134). The persistence of German balances of payments surpluses were increasingly based upon their ability to depress wages growth.[10] The accumulation of these surpluses translated into an increase in foreign investment and bank lending to the deficit countries of the periphery. Since monetary policy was set by the ECB and fiscal policy was constrained by the Maastricht Treaty, the peripheral countries not only experienced a deflationary adjustment, but were compelled to improve their international export competitiveness by savagely curtailing wages growth as well. It was, therefore, not too surprising that the peripheral states have become more reliant on private foreign borrowings from the core countries in order to finance their respective fiscal deficits (Lucarelli, 2011–12). As Bibow notes:

> Starting from near zero net foreign assets in the late 1990s, Germany's creditor position reached 40 per cent of GDP by the end of 2010. Not only has Germany's net foreign asset position improved so markedly, the introduction of the euro has also seen a sharp rise in gross cross-border positions – reflecting surging gross capital flows of all kinds (FDI, portfolio equity, potfolio debt and other investments, the latter including bank loans). (2012, p.25)

Similarly, exchange rate re-alignments were simply not possible within the currency union, despite continued divergences in inflation and interest rates (Pivetti, 1998, p.16). Deprived of the conventional fiscal and

DOI: 10.1057/9781137371904

exchange rate policy instruments on the supranational level, the eurozone could only attempt to resolve these internal imbalances through the repression of wages and policies of competitive disinflation. With the irrevocable fixing of exchange rates, which prefigured the birth of the euro, the international competitiveness of the deficit countries has been gradually eroded over the past two decades. Many of these countries were condemned to evolve as the peripheral satellite states of Germany. Since Germany pursued a neo-mercantilist policy characterised by competitive disinflation, the deficit countries, in the absence of exchange rate policy, were compelled to pursue a similar strategy in order to prevent the loss of their export competitiveness. While the surplus countries, most notably Germany, enjoyed lower interest rates on their issuing of sovereign debt, the deficit countries were confronted by a vicious circle of higher interest rates, credit downgrading and higher exposure to the risk of default, which pushed them into an unsustainable debt trap (Nersisyan and Wray, 2010, p.17). Quite contrary to the Maastricht objectives of convergence, these imbalances between the deficit and surplus countries have diverged quite substantially and have imparted a whole series of asymmetrical shocks within the eurozone.

Since fiscal policy was constrained, member states have resorted to the promotion of exports to compensate for the lack of domestic effective demand. The great danger of pursuing a neo-mercantilist strategy, however, was the spectre of triggering a series of "beggar thy neighbour" policies from foreign rivals (Sardoni and Wray, 2006, p.469). This over-reliance on foreign demand as the engine of growth could lead to the outbreak of retaliatory trade wars as each country pursues "a desperate expedient to maintain employment at home by forcing sales in foreign markets and restricting purchases, which, if successful, will merely shift the problem of unemployment to the neighbor" (Keynes, 1936, pp.382–83). Within the eurozone, however, the maintenance of irrevocably fixed exchange rates implied that the only means by which to improve international competitiveness was through wage repression and policies of competitive disinflation. Indeed, one of the ubiquitous legacies of this process of competitive disinflation has been the persistence of high levels of unemployment and chronic problems of excess productive capacity, which have inhibited the self-reinforcing effects of the investment multiplier. It is possible to foresee that this prolonged phase of disinflation could eventually push the eurozone into a depressive spiral, characterised by a debilitating phase of debt-deflation (Lapavitsas, *et al.*,

DOI: 10.1057/9781137371904

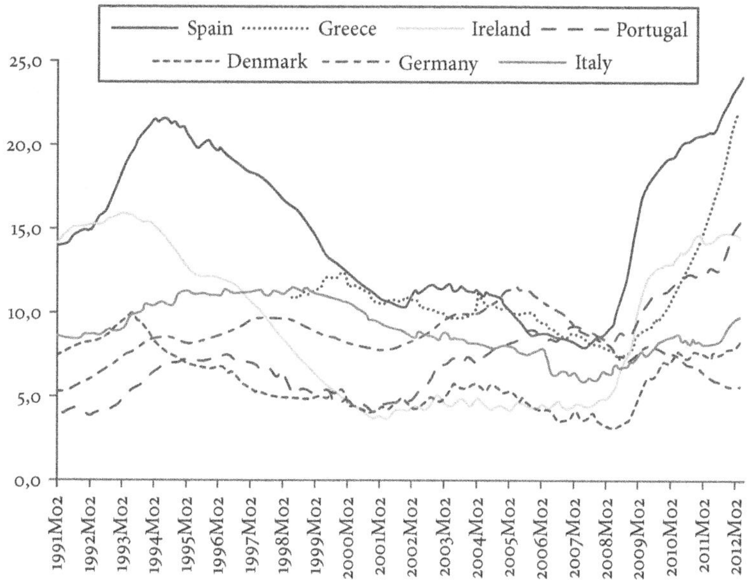

FIGURE 7.4 *Unemployment in the EU, selected countries, 1991–2012*
Source: http://www.economonitor.com/blog/2011/12/which-graph-best-summarizes-theeurozone-crisis.

2010, p.73). Figure 7.4 summarises these negative trends in unemployment rates.

Consequently, at the very epicentre of this deflationary spiral has been the role performed by Germany. The growing divergence between burgeoning German trade surpluses and the trade deficits of the peripheral countries threatened the internal coherence of the eurozone.[11] Moreover, the reluctance of the German authorities to stimulate the level of effective demand has imparted a powerful deflationary impulse throughout the eurozone (Bibow, 2006, p.33). However, as export markets began to evaporate as a result of the international recession of 2008–10, the deficit countries encountered the limits of this neo-mercantilist strategy of export-led growth. On the other hand, Germany was capable of overcoming these limits imposed by the lack of effective demand domestically and in the eurozone. Germany's export surpluses to the US and East Asia have to a large extent compensated for the loss of markets in Europe. But the persistence of stagnant and declining real wages in Germany has spilled-over into the rest of the eurozone as each country pursued similar neo-mercantilist policies. Wage repression in Germany has therefore set in motion a "race to the bottom" within the eurozone (Carchedi, 1997, pp.100–1). Confronted by wage competition from East Asia, these policies of wage repression continued to reinforce Europe's longstanding structural decline. Most of the peripheral deficit countries have encountered quite savage competition and a loss of markets from low-wage Asian countries (Roubini, 2010, p.1). The real appreciation of the euro over the previous decade – itself partly the result of disinflation and tight monetary policies by the ECB – contributed to this loss of international competitiveness.[12]

Conclusion

If current policies of fiscal austerity continue to inform the macroeconomic stance of the governments of the eurozone, it is quite possible that the peripheral deficit countries could experience a prolonged phase of debt-deflation. In this worst case scenario, the onset of deflation could set in motion a chain of events that could lead to the cessation of debt validation and the emergence of a severe economic slump. A cascading series of sovereign debt defaults could set in train this cumulative process of stagnation and decline. Consequently, the liquidation of debts acts as both a cause and a catalyst for the onset of debt-deflation. The more that debtors attempt to validate their obligations, the more difficult it becomes to liquidate their assets because of falling prices (Fischer, 1933). Under these extreme circumstances, monetary policy becomes entirely ineffectual with the emergence of a pervasive liquidity trap, similar to the Japanese experience over the past two decades. The possible onset of a deflationary trap in the peripheral countries would, in turn, have a detrimental effect in terms of a concomitant diminution of effective demand for the exports and investment of the core, surplus countries of the eurozone. At the same time, the descent into a phase of debt-deflation will merely limit the ability of these peripheral countries to service their burgeoning debt. In the final analysis, the chronic current account deficits and the sovereign debt crises engulfing Greece, Portugal, Spain, Ireland and possibly Italy – ultimately reflects the failure of the neoliberal design of the Maastricht Treaty to achieve greater regional convergence and the creation of a supranational fiscal regime. There is a very real likelihood that these peripheral countries could eventually default on their respective sovereign debt and exit the eurozone. Indeed,

DOI: 10.1057/9781137371904

the powerful centrifugal forces unleashed by the neoliberal strategy of "negative integration" could prefigure the eventual disintegration of the EU itself.

Notes

1 The funds provided by the IMF originated from the contributions of member states, which have only increased the public debt ratios of these very same member states.

2 Greece will face very high debt repayments by 2014–15 when its repayments increase from €40–50 billion to €70 billion. At the same time, the shortfall in revenues because of the prolonged recession will make it difficult to achieve its deficit reduction targets.

3 In both the Treaties of Maastricht and Amsterdam, and enshrined in the Statute of the European System of Central Banks (ESCB) and the Charter of the ECB, the role of lender of last resort is omitted entirely (Spethmann and Steiger, 2004, p.61).

4 The recent Treaty of Lisbon, which was ratified in 2009, enshrines the independence of the ECB and price stability as the primary objective of monetary policy (Cesaratto, 2010, p.1).

5 Estimates of the dampening effects on the output gap by Eichengreen and Wyplosz (1998) suggest that "After accumulation over the past 2 decades, levels of real output would have ended 5 per cent lower in France and the UK and 9 per cent lower in Italy" (1998, p.68).

6 The basic rationale of functional finance is best summarized by Lerner: "The central idea is that government fiscal policy, its spending and taxing, its borrowing and repayment of loans, its issue of new money and its withdrawal of money, shall all be undertaken with an eye only in the *results* of these actions in the economy and not to any established traditional doctrine about what is sound or unsound. This principle of judging only by the *effects* has been applied in many other fields of human activity, where it is known as the method of science as opposed to scholasticism. The principle of judging fiscal measures by the way they work or function in the economy we may call *functional finance*" (1943, p.39).

7 The ECB *indirectly* monetises the public debt through open-market operations in the secondary bond markets. However, the ECB has been prohibited from issuing Eurobonds to finance these public debts.

8 The introduction of the euro has paradoxically prevented the Bundesbank from sterilising the inflow of US dollars in order to mitigate the effects of exchange rate appreciation and maintain their export competitiveness. The

DOI: 10.1057/9781137371904

appreciation of the euro over the past decade has therefore had a negative effect on German export competitiveness. These unfavourable trends have only further intensified German neo-mercantilist austerity and domestic wage repression.

9 Germany has recently been able to divert their exports and investment to the booming Chinese market. In 2010, Spain, Portugal and Greece absorbed only about 7 per cent of total German exports (Bellofiore, *et al.*, 2010, p.137).

10 According to Bellofiore *et al.* (2010, p.135): "Between 2000 and 2008, German labour productivity had grown by more than 35% of the European average, while real wages lagged labour productivity growth."

11 The German trade surplus increased from 2.8 per cent of GDP in 2000 to 7 per cent of GDP in 2008 (Cesaratto, 2010, p.3).

12 Between the beginning of 2002 and November 2007, the dollar had depreciated by more than 50 per cent against the euro.

DOI: 10.1057/9781137371904

8

The Break-Up of the Eurozone?

Abstract: *The centrifugal dynamics set in train by the neoliberal strategy of "negative integration" have set the stage for the disintegration of the eurozone in its current incarnation.1 Still in its early phases, this process of dissolution could threaten the very foundations of the post-war European project and could generate unpredictable political and social turmoil as popular sentiment clamours for the restoration of the primacy of national sovereignty. Despite the massive bailouts imposed on the peripheral, deficit countries, a dangerous feedback loop has emerged in which the banking crisis has morphed into successive sovereign debt crises. The subsequent austerity measures have merely pushed the eurozone into a vicious circle of falling government revenue caused by the recession, which in turn, has only further increased their respective debt burden (Backburn, 2011, p.39). But the onset of a fiscal crisis has provoked a downgrading of the creditworthiness of the debtor states and triggered further speculative attacks in the bond markets as government bond yields increased sharply.*

Lucarelli, Bill. *Endgame for the Euro: A Critical History.* Basingtoke: Palgrave Macmillan, 2013.
DOI: 10.1057/9781137371904.

Introduction

The centrifugal dynamics set in train by the neoliberal strategy of "negative integration" have set the stage for the disintegration of the eurozone in its current incarnation.[2] Still in its early phases, this process of dissolution could threaten the very foundations of the post-war European project and could generate unpredictable political and social turmoil as popular sentiment clamours for the restoration of the primacy of national sovereignty. Since the outbreak of the debt crisis, large-scale bail-outs by the IMF/EU/ECB (Troika) have been imposed on Ireland, Greece, Portugal and Spain. Despite these massive bailouts, a dangerous feedback loop has emerged in which the banking crisis has morphed into successive sovereign debt crises. The subsequent austerity measures have merely pushed the eurozone into a vicious circle of falling government revenue caused by the recession, which in turn, has only further increased their respective debt burden (Blackburn, 2011, p.39). But the onset of a fiscal crisis provoked a downgrading of the creditworthiness of the debtor states and triggered further speculative attacks in the bond markets as government bond yields increased sharply.

This perilous embrace between the bond markets and sovereign states creates further uncertainty and volatility as global investors frantically take flight into safe havens. The flight into US Treasury bonds has witnessed US yields falling to their lowest levels in 60 years. In the absence of fiscal solidarity embodied by the creation of a European Treasury, the survival of the euro in its present form could be imperilled by this dangerously self-reinforcing logic between these speculative bond markets and the onset of a "depressive spiral" imposed through austerity on those countries encountering severe debt crises. At the same time, the member states have attempted to mitigate the effects of contagion in the event of a possible default by the deficit countries through the creation of several short-term financing facilities and by attempting to overcome the Maastricht Treaty's prohibition of the ECB acting as a lender of last resort. The extent to which these measures can ameliorate the impending sovereign debt crises will also be examined in this chapter.

The Dominoes tumble

The magnitude of the slump engulfing the peripheral states is summarised in Table 8.1. Greece received a Troika bail-out in May 2010,

DOI: 10.1057/9781137371904

followed by Ireland in November 2010 and Portugal in May 2011. Celebrated as the "Celtic tiger", Ireland attracted an enormous inflow of foreign investment in the decades preceding the crisis as it re-invented itself as a dynamic information technology hub. Leading high technology multinational corporations were lured by generous tax concessions and a skilled workforce, which transformed Ireland into an export platform. At the same time, Ireland also became a major offshore financial centre as successive governments enacted policies of financial deregulation. The boom spilled-over into the property market as the Irish banking sector over-invested in the real estate market, fuelling an unprecedented property bubble. The over-heating construction sector had accounted for about 23 per cent of GNP by 2007 (Finn, 2011, p.11). At the end of 2003, the net foreign indebtedness of Irish banks was estimated at 10 per cent of GDP. By early 2008, this figure had increased dramatically to over 60 per cent of GDP (Kitromolides, 2012, p.170).

After the collapse of the property market, the Irish banking system was effectively insolvent. In late 2008, the government intervened with a recapitalisation plan worth €3.5 billion for Ireland's three major commercial banks: Allied Irish Bank, Bank of Ireland and Anglo Irish Bank. This blanket guarantee for the banking system inevitably caused the sovereign debt crisis as the budget deficit and public debt exploded. From a balanced budget in 2007, the Irish fiscal deficit increased to 14 per cent of GDP in 2009. The Irish government had guaranteed €785bn of Irish and foreign bank liabilities. These toxic assets were now purchased by the National Asset and Management Agency (NAMA) in exchange for government bonds. In short, the bad debts of the banks and developers were socialised (McArthur, 2011, p.48). The eventual bail-out of the Irish banks by the Troika in November 2010 was estimated at €130bn. In the wake of the bail-out, the government imposed a severe programme of austerity, which represented the largest spending cuts in the history of the Irish Republic.[3]

The next domino to fall was Greece.[4] Between 2007 and 2009, the Greek budget deficit increased from 6.4 per cent to 15 per cent of GDP. As speculation on an impending Greek default intensified, eurozone leaders agreed to a €130bn bail-out deal but have demanded that the loan would be conditional on the Greek government enacting quite savage austerity measures. In return for the loan, the Socialist government agreed to reduce the public debt to 120 per cent of GDP by 2020. Private bondholders were forced to accept a "hair cut" of 53 per cent of the face value of their Greek government bonds in the bond swap engineered

DOI: 10.1057/9781137371904

by the Troika. The outstanding 85 per cent of Greek government debt, equivalent to €280bn was to be held by the ECB, the European Financial Stability Fund (EFSF), the IMF, as well as by Greek state pensions and its banks (Christie, 2012, p.16). Indeed, the Troika's intervention was motivated almost entirely by the threat of financial contagion to the rest of the eurozone in the event of a Greek default. Under these circumstances, it was necessary to declare that the loss to bondholders was voluntary and that the agreement would allow new loans to be issued to Greece on the condition that the Greek government would implement severe austerity measures (Lapavitsas, 2012).

Despite official denials, the Greek government effectively defaulted on its debts to private bondholders, estimated at €173bn. The so-called voluntary agreement was negotiated with Europe's banks, pension funds and hedge funds. What ultimately prevented a full-scale default was the swap agreement with bondholders to switch their holdings to 30-year maturities in which they were guaranteed a return of 3–5 per cent per annum by the EFSF. By late 2011, the eurozone debt crisis had escalated and threatened to engulf the larger economies of Spain and Italy. The Greek socialist Prime Minister announced plans for a referendum over

TABLE 8.1 *Economic indicators for Greece, Ireland, Portugal and Spain, 2002–11*

Countries Economic indicators	2002	2004	2006	2008	2009	2010	2011
Greece (a)	3.4	4.4	4.6	−0.14	−3.3	−3.5	−6.9
(b)	10.3	10.5	8.9	7.7	9.4	12.5	17.3
(c)	−6.5	−5.8	−11.2	−14.7	−11.0	−10.0	−9.7
(d)	85.5	98.8	106.1	110.7	127.1	142.7	163.3
Ireland (a)	5.8	4.5	5.3	−3.0	−7.0	−0.43	0.
(b)	4.4	4.5	4.4	6.3	11.8	13.6	14.4
(c)	−1.0	−0.6	−3.5	−5.7	−3.0	0.5	0.1
(d)	25.0	19.8	12.1	24.5	42.2	76.9	96.0
Portugal (a)	0.8	1.6	1.5	0	−3.0	1.4	−1.5
(b)	5.1	6.6	7.7	7.6	9.5	10.8	12.7
(c)	−8.2	−8.3	−10.7	−12.6	−10.9	−10.0	−6.4
(d)	48	53.1	58.6	67.4	78.8	89.2	100.4
Spain (a)	2.7	3.3	4.1	0.9	−3.7	−0.07	0.7
(b)	11.5	11.0	8.5	11.3	18.0	20.1	21.6
(c)	−3.4	−5.2	−9.0	−9.6	−5.2	−4.6	−3.7
(d)	44.0	38.6	30.7	30.8	42.5	49.7	56.9

(a) GDP (constant prices); (b) Unemployment (% of workforce); (c) Current Account Balance (% of GDP); (d) Net Government Debt (% of GDP)
Source: IMF Statistics, 2012.

the punitive and harsh terms of the bail-out agreed at the European Summit in October. After the G-20 Summit in Cannes on 4 November, the plan for a national referendum was abandoned after opposition from the French President Sarkozy and German Chancellor Merkel. Papandreou resigned two days later and on 10 November, Papademos, a former President of the Bank of Greece and Vice President of the ECB, was installed as the new Prime Minister of a national unity government formed by the conservatives and socialists. This Greek drama had now turned into a tragic farce. In the country that had invented the very idea of democracy witnessed its temporary suspension by the financial oligarchy.

The overall effect of the austerity programme was devastating. After signing the Memorandum of Agreement with the Troika, salaries and pensions were cut by a quarter and public spending slashed in order to secure an initial €110bn loan. The unemployment rate skyrocketed to more than 24 per cent in 2012, whilst GDP plunged by -3.3 per cent in 2009, -3.5 per cent in 2010 and -6.9 per cent in 2011 as Greece descended into a deep depression (Kouvelakis, 2011, p.23). The very wealthy escaped taxation through tax loopholes and offshore tax havens, while most of the burden of taxation was imposed on public sector employees. Indeed, under the system of "clientelism", the growth of public sector employment had disguised the underlying structural problems of rampant tax avoidance. The logic was quite perverse and self-reinforcing: increasing public sector employment had merely reinforced the state's dependence on public sector tax revenue, which then encouraged the very growth of unproductive public sector employment itself. Widespread tax avoidance by the private sector reinforced this logic and promoted the "regulatory capture" of private enterprises through the various public subsidies and tax concessions. In other words, the whole system of mutual private-public clientelism reproduced a network of cronyism and state support for unproductive private sector employment known as "diaploki" in Greece (Pitellis, 2012, pp.81–82). This intricate web of corruption and patronage formed the very core of the Greek political system in which productive investment was discouraged. The system bred a culture of redistribution and corruption. The size of the Greek underground economy accounted for an estimated 30 per cent of GDP, while services and tourism represented over 73 per cent of GDP (Karagiannis and Kondeas, 2012, p.58). Ultimately, the savage cut-backs in government spending swelled the

DOI: 10.1057/9781137371904

ranks of the unemployed and through the automatic stabilisers, led to a collapse in government revenue and spiralling net public debt.

Portugal was also drawn into the maelstrom of the debt crisis engulfing the peripheral countries. After an impressive phase of economic expansion in the years preceding the birth of the euro in 1999, Portugal's current account deficit blew out to over 12.6 per cent of GDP in 2008. The excessive growth of domestic effective demand contributed to the worsening external balance as Portugal's real effective exchange rate (REER) was highly over-valued when Portugal entered the eurozone. Portugal's higher rate of inflation relative to Germany translated into lower real interest rates set by the ECB, which induced high levels of private debt and ignited a real estate boom (Lead and Palacio-Vera, 2012, p.203). This structural problem continued to deteriorate over the first decade of Portugal's entry into the eurozone with unemployment rising to 15.4 per cent in June 2012. At the same time, net public debt increased inexorably to exceed 100 per cent of GDP in 2011. In response to these burgeoning twin deficits, successive governments embarked upon a programme of severe austerity. By May 2011, the Troika approved a bail-out worth €78bn. Under the terms of this bail-out, Portugal agreed to reduce its budget deficit to 4.5 per cent of GDP in 2012 and 3 per cent in 2013. In 2011, the ruling conservative government reduced the budget deficit of 7.7 per cent to 4.2 per cent of GDP by simply transferring state pension assets from the domestic banks. Despite severe cut-backs in government spending and increased taxes, the fiscal target of 4.5 per cent of GDP was not achieved in 2012.

Given the relative size of Spain as the fourth largest in the eurozone, the impending fiscal crisis poses an existential threat to the entire Eurosystem. In the decade 1996 to 2007, Spain experienced a rapid expansion of GDP, estimated at 51.5 per cent in real terms. Much of this boom, however, was driven by excessive investment in the financial sector and in private construction. For instance, the construction sector grew from 7.8 per cent to 9.5 per cent of GDP between 1997 and 2007, while the finance sector, which financed the real estate boom, had expanded from 18.3 per cent to 22.3 per cent of GDP over the same period (Ferreiro and Serrano, 2012, p.240). At the same time, the level of aggregate demand expanded even faster than the growth of real GDP. Similar to the Portuguese experience, this excessive growth of domestic demand led to the blow-out of Spain's current account deficit. From a small surplus of 0.5 per cent of GDP in 1997, the trade deficit reached 10.4 per cent of GDP in 2007.

The massive inflow of capital, which financed this real estate boom, was reflected in the extraordinary increase in Spain's foreign debt. If one excludes direct investment, the external debt increased from €253 bn or 53.4 per cent of GDP in 2006 to an estimated €1.8 trillion or equivalent to 171.4 per cent of GDP in 2009. The external debt generated by foreign borrowings by domestic banks accounted for 116 per cent of GDP in 2007 (Ferreiro and Serrano, 2012, p.253). The eventual crash of Spain's property market in the wake of the global financial crisis of 2007–08 caused a prolonged economic slump from which it has yet to recover.

The neoliberal policies enacted by the Spanish Socialist government during its 14-year rule (1982–96) included mass privatisations, the liberalisation of the telecommunications and energy sectors, the deregulation of the labour market and the severe cut-backs in government spending. These policies led to a weakening of the "automatic" fiscal stabilisers as the relative size of the public sector was curtailed, which caused the budget deficit to deteriorate quite rapidly during the severe recession of 2009–10. At the same time, the large-scale recapitalisation of Spain's largest banks also contributed to Spain's burgeoning fiscal crisis. From a small budget surplus of 1.9 per cent of GDP in 2005, Spain's budget deficit reached 11.1 per cent of GDP in 2009 (Polychroniou, 2012, p.9). Spain's 17 autonomous regional governments, which provide essential services like education and health, have experienced quite serious financial distress with many of them in a state of technical default after the massive recapitalisation of the banking system. The new austerity programme introduced in September 2012 has prolonged Spain's deep recession as unemployment exceeded 25 per cent. In mid-2012, the Spanish government reluctantly accepted a €100bn European bail-out of insolvent Spanish banks.

Greece, Spain and Portugal share a common historical lineage. All three countries experienced a post-dictatorship democratic revival and were quite recent in their respective gravitation as peripheral and subaltern states into the orbit of Europe's northern growth poles. Their peripheral status within the European division of labour has limited their development as advanced capitalist social formations, while their political institutions continued to be governed by regimes of patronage and clientelism. The lack of open and transparent political institutions has been characterised by highly inefficient and corrupt public bureaucracies. Rampant tax evasion and the close ties between the upper echelons of the state with the dominant business interests have created a political

DOI: 10.1057/9781137371904

TABLE 8.2 *Private sector debt as a percentage of GDP, 1995–2008*

	Households		Businesses	
	1995	2008	1995	2008
Greece	13	61	38	62
Portugal	42	108	53	134
Spain	42	88	47	122

Source: Milios and Sotiropoulos, 2010, p.232.

culture of vested interests, which has stifled the demands for democratic renewal. The pathologies of "crony capitalism" contributed to the massive waste associated with corruption and the propagation of social inequalities and persistently high rates of poverty. Under these political circumstances, the imposition of quite harsh neoliberal policies merely perpetuated these social contradictions and exacerbated the growing debt crises that have engulfed these peripheral states. In the words of Polychroniou:

> As such, the debt crisis in the eurozone periphery is as much political as it is economic, and problems facing countries like Greece, Portugal and Spain are related as much to the macroeconomic environment created by their domestic regimes as to the flawed architecture of the euro-system and Germany's aggressive export policies. The regressive policies these countries adopted during the past 2 to 3 decades produced macroeconomic environments that were extremely weak, lacking a foundation for sustainable growth and job creation, and loaded with all kinds of social contradictions. (2012, p.10)

Quite apart from their burgeoning public debts, the accumulation of private debt has been even more pernicious in these peripheral countries. Table 8.2 summarises the growth in private sector debt in the countries of Greece, Portugal and Spain during the years 1995 to 2008.

The "dance of death" between states and markets

Between 1999 and 2008, before the outbreak of the global financial crisis, household debt in the eurozone increased from about 50 to 70 per cent, while the increase in bank debt was even more severe, estimated at 250 per cent of the combined eurozone GDP in 2008. During the

DOI: 10.1057/9781137371904

same period, public debt had fallen from an average of 72 per cent to 68 per cent of the combined eurozone GDP (De Grauwe, 2010, p.1). In the wake of the global financial crisis of 2008–09, the ensuing credit crunch witnessed a severe process of deleveraging by the private banks in order to restore their respective balance sheets. Most governments in the eurozone attempted to counter the liquidity crisis by pursuing more expansionary fiscal and monetary policies. At the same time, the massive bail-outs of the private banks by national governments also led inexorably to burgeoning fiscal deficits. The onset of recession and growing unemployment merely served to increase these national budget deficits through the operation of automatic stabilisers. In short, the private debt had now morphed into escalating government deficits. An excellent summary is provided by Arestis and Sawyer:

> In terms of competitiveness (as measured by unit labour costs), Greece, Ireland, Portugal and Spain have lost 25–30 per cent since the creation of the EMU in January 1999. The current account deficits of the south European countries required these countries to borrow heavily from other countries, and from north European banks as well as British and American ones. Because south European countries had much lower interest rates than previously, they rapidly built up their debt. The debts were mainly, though not exclusively, private sector rather than public sector. However, when the Great Recession hit, borrowing was increasingly done by government. (2011, pp.7–8)

The ultimate irony was that as soon as the threat of a sovereign debt default emerged, bond markets began to demand higher risk premiums reflected in higher yields for public borrowings. In the absence of financial solidarity in the event of a sell-off of government bonds, the entire eurozone became vulnerable to escalating bond yields and rising interest rates. The flight from the high deficit countries to the low deficit/surplus countries was reflected in diverging bond yields within the eurozone (Figure 8.1). This self-reinforcing dynamic has parallels with the ERM crisis of 1992 in the sense that the failure of governments to maintain exchange rate parities triggered the subsequent speculative attacks (Lucarelli, 2004a). Under the euro, however, exchange rate devaluations were not possible. The exchange rate crisis now became a sovereign debt crisis in which bond markets encountered the threat of a devaluation of government bonds. The spectre of contagion caused by cascading sovereign debt defaults threatened the very survival of the eurozone.

DOI: 10.1057/9781137371904

It can be surmised that the crisis in the eurozone was more a banking crisis than a sovereign debt crisis. Indeed, the crisis might be one of solvency rather than liquidity in which most of the non-performing loans incurred during the crash of 2008, have yet to be cleansed from the balance sheets of the banks themselves. Interbank lending has contracted quite sharply as the commercial paper market begins to evaporate. A liquidity trap could also emerge in the wake of the desperate attempts by banks and firms to deleverage and restore their respective balance sheets. A vicious circle has been set in train as risk premiums demanded by the banks to purchase government bonds escalated (Soros, 2012, p.86). This negative feedback loop only further aggravated the sovereign debt crisis in a self-reinforcing logic. In order to circumvent this vicious circle, the ECB has attempted to intervene in secondary bond markets to ease the pressure of rising bond yields on government re-financing operations. But the question of how the costs and funding for these bail-outs were to be shared between national governments became critical (James, 2009, p.217). In the absence of fiscal federalism or a common European Treasury, the German government has doubtless been very reluctant to incur the main burden of financing these operations.

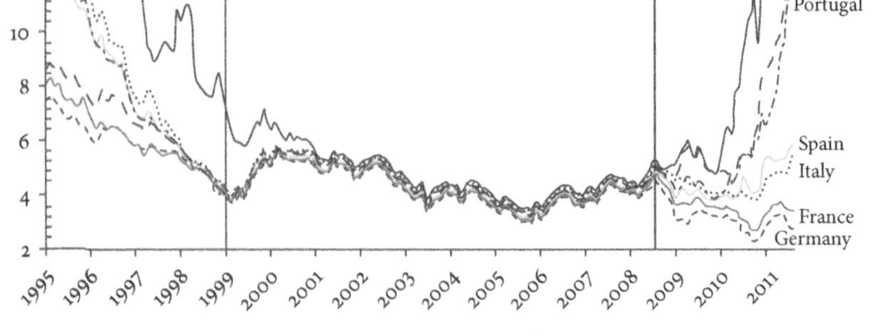

FIGURE 8.1 *Interest rates on 10-year government bonds (%)*

Source: http://www.economonitor.com/blog/2011/12/which-graph-best-summarizes-theeurozone-crisis.

which will acquire the role of providing external financial assistance to distressed member states of the eurozone after June 2013. Access to these funds, however, were conditional on the recipient governments imposing austerity and wage repression (Hein, *et al.*, 2012, p.37). Critics have argued that these funds were not adequately capitalised and their functions have been confined to temporary, short-term interventions. Indeed, in late 2011, these financial resources amounted only to €440bn, which were inadequate to bail-out the larger countries of Spain and Italy in the event of a sovereign default (Lapavitsas, *et al.*, 2011, p.32). In other words, as Soros has argued, the proposed ESM fell short of evolving into an embryonic common Treasury (Soros, 2012, pp.126–27). The other major shortcoming was that the existing EFSF was only a fund-raising mechanism and the authority to spend money was governed by the short-term needs of member states rather than acting as an automatic mechanism that could be deployed in the event of cascading sovereign defaults.

The EFSF and the design of the future ESM resembled the notorious Special Purpose Vehicles (SPVs) that allowed banks to remove their toxic assets from their balance sheets during the subprime crisis in the US. As a private, independent entity, the EFSF has been given the power to issue bonds in the capital markets in order to raise funds to bail-out sovereign states encountering the threat of default. At the same time, these bonds issued by the EFSF were guaranteed by the European member states based upon their respective capital contributions to the ECB. The market for these bonds included the IMF and the surplus countries with large foreign exchange reserves such as the wealthy OPEC states, Japan and the so-called BRIC countries (Brazil, Russia, India and China). During the Euro-summit in July 2012, member states (with the exception of Germany) eventually succumbed to pressure by Spain and Italy to provide financial assistance through the EFSF/ESM in order to recapitalise their commercial banks and support their government bonds *without* having to submit to the onerous Troika programme of austerity that had already been imposed on Greece, Portugal and Ireland. This imposition of austerity would now be the sole preserve of national governments. The summit also agreed to establish a single banking supervisor for the eurozone as a whole. The ESM would have a banking licence that would allow the ECB to issue three-year loans to the ESM and support its financing operations. In other words, Italy and Spain would acquire access to unlimited funds via the ECB. Although trenchantly opposed by

DOI: 10.1057/9781137371904

the German representatives of the summit, this agreement culminated in the Draghi Plan, announced in September 2012, which effectively codified the ECB's de facto role as lender of last resort.[6]

In short, Germany and other eurozone countries with a triple-A bond rating, had now reluctantly agreed to support the deficit countries and avoid the possible breakdown of the eurozone. Ultimately, the survival of the euro will depend upon Germany's willingness to support the ECB/ESM mechanism. The fate of the euro therefore increasingly rests upon the domestic political support within Germany, which continues to be very hostile to the idea that Germany should extend credit to the deficit countries. Given this political reality, the dynamics of disintegration within Europe will gain momentum only over the next few years. The real Achilles's heel of the existing eurozone banking system is the inter-bank transfer of deposits, known as the TARGET-2 (Trans-European Automated Real Time Gross Settlement Express Transfer System) facility, which allows the automatic and costless transfer of deposits from one bank to another within the eurozone. The possible breakdown of the European financial system could be provoked by a stampede out of deposits in the peripheral states into the safe haven of high yielding deposits in German banks (Papadimitriou and Wray, 2012, p.2). This scenario could trigger a major banking crisis and could quite easily prefigure the eventual demise of the euro project.

Conclusion

The survival of the existing euro-system appears to be increasingly problematic. The internal contradictions between the core surplus countries and the peripheral deficit countries threaten the very existence of the euro in its present form. These centrifugal and discordant elements could eventually destroy the whole post-war European project. The dangerously self-fulfilling logic between these speculative bond markets and the cascading, deflationary spiral imposed on those countries encountering severe debt crises resembled the worst features of the inter-war gold standard that was eventually abandoned in the early 1930s. At present it might be premature to declare its eventual demise. In this context, the rather piecemeal and ad hoc responses to the crisis so far might prolong the life span of the euro for a while yet, perhaps several more years. In the absence of political union and fiscal federalism, however, the future of the euro appears to be quite bleak. The problem is essentially political.

DOI: 10.1057/9781137371904

At the core of its resolution lies the willingness of Germany to accept the burden of financing the deficit countries and undertaking a sustained programme of expansionary fiscal policies to counter-act the tendencies toward economic stagnation and the possible onset of a debilitating phase of debt-deflation. This implies no less than a type of European Marshall Plan via fiscal federalism to re-activate growth and economic reconstruction. At present, the likelihood of such an ambitious programme would appear to be very remote.

Notes

1. The process of European integration has been characterised by a gradual transfer of national sovereignty over the economic and political instruments of state power to an emergent supranational regime of governance. Negative integration implies that the process of economic integration should prefigure political union. The whole process is ostensibly governed by the dynamic of economic "spill-over". In other words, as strategic sectors of the national economy come under the auspices of supranational institutions, the logic of cumulative causation will impel member states to relinquish their national sovereignty over other related sectors of the economy. Enshrined by the Single Market Act of 1987 and the Maastricht Treaty of 1992, the neoliberal strategy of negative integration sought to abolish all existing barriers to the free movement of goods, services, labour and capital across national frontiers.
2. The process of European integration has been characterised by a gradual transfer of national sovereignty over the economic and political instruments of state power to an emergent supranational regime of governance. Negative integration implies that the process of economic integration should prefigure political union. The whole process is ostensibly governed by the dynamic of economic "spill-over". In other words, as strategic sectors of the national economy come under the auspices of supranational institutions, the logic of cumulative causation will impel member states to relinquish their national sovereignty over other related sectors of the economy. Enshrined by the Single Market Act of 1987 and the Maastricht Treaty of 1992, the neoliberal strategy of negative integration sought to abolish all existing barriers to the free movement of goods, services, labour and capital across national frontiers.
3. According to McArthur: "With an interest rate of 5.8 per cent in the ECB-IMF bail-out package, interest payments alone on the state debt will be more than 20 per cent of tax revenues in 2014" (2011, p.45).

DOI: 10.1057/9781137371904

4 A very succinct summary of Greece's fall from financial grace is provided by Norfield (2012): "All the evidence shows that the Greek debt crisis has been long in the making. The root causes were a mixture of widespread tax-evasion, the misuse (since the 1980s) of EU development funds to finance current government spending, a private-sector credit-boom based on borrowing rates not far above Germany's after joining EMU in 2001, and declining competitiveness. The Greek government – assisted by Goldman Sachs and other banks – used derivatives to hide its weak finances and qualify for EMU" (pp.124–25).

5 According to Arestis and Sawyer (2012): "There is a well-known accounting relationship of (G – T) = (Q – X) + (S – I) (where G is government expenditure, T tax revenues, Q imports, X exports plus net income from abroad, S private savings and I private investment). The scale of the budget deficit (or indeed budget surplus) then depends on the size of the current account deficit, private savings and investment at a high level of economic activity. It then follows that the appropriate budget deficit depends on the conditions surrounding the current account (propensities to import, exports) and the net savings position (savings – investment). For a country with a current account deficit and a tendency for savings to exceed investment would require a large budget deficit, while in contrast for a country with a current account surplus, and investment to exceed saving, a large budget surplus would be appropriate" (p.17).

6 The aim of the ECB's plan to buy sovereign bonds in secondary bond markets was to ease fears over the threat of country default and lower the bond yields in order to allow the indebted peripheral countries to service their debts. The ECB could also "sterilise" its purchases to avoid re-igniting inflationary pressures. In other words, these open market operations were offset by reducing the issuing of euros from circulation. The operation – known as the Outright Monetary Transaction – was eventually approved by the German Constitutional Court on 12 September 2012.

DOI: 10.1057/9781137371904

Conclusion

Lucarelli, Bill. *Endgame for the Euro: A Critical History.* Basingtoke: Palgrave Macmillan, 2013.
DOI: 10.1057/9781137371904.

Conceived as a response to the breakdown of the post-war Bretton Woods accords, the euro project is now at the threshold of disintegration as the fault-lines between the core/surplus countries and the peripheral/deficit countries experience a profound rupture. In the absence of political union and fiscal federalism, these centrifugal forces appear to be irreversible. Either the peripheral states default and exit the euro, or Germany itself comes to the conclusion that the existing burden of financing the deficit countries can no longer be justified and declares its intention to construct its own exclusive currency bloc or simply restores the DM to its pre-eminent role. There are, of course, several other scenarios in between these two extremes that might involve the creation of a new informal monetary architecture resembling an intra-European payments union in which the euro is declared non-convertible except as a unit of account between central banks. Whatever the final outcome, it is difficult to envisage the current system, plagued as it is by internal contradictions, surviving the crisis that now engulfs the entire eurozone. The present crisis is to a large extent the continuation of the longstanding neoliberal policies favoured by Germany, which have informed the creation of the euro. This study has examined the historical context and the theoretical debates that have animated the long and tortuous political process in the construction of this flawed monetary edifice. A brief summary of this history might provide invaluable insights. Several future scenarios will also be explored.

The emergence of trans-Atlantic trade rivalry signalled a decisive moment in the origins of a zone of monetary stability in Europe. Economic rivalry was triggered by the onset of the dollar crisis and the unprecedented inflow of US direct investment in the EEC during the 1960s. The American challenge evoked fears in Europe of the spectre of industrial colonisation and induced a wave of mergers and corporate take-overs in Europe in order to counter the US corporate invasion. At the same time, the demise of the post-war system of fixed exchange rates had provoked a series of exchange rate crises, which threatened to undermine the Common Market. In response, European leaders sought to create a zone of monetary stability within Europe. As the international economic crisis intensified in the early 1970s, it became increasingly evident that the loss of national sovereignty over economic policies could be recovered on a supranational level.

> In this sense, one may say that the movement towards Western European economic integration via the Common Market is a product of capitalist penetration on an international scale: an attempt by capitalism to reconcile

DOI: 10.1057/9781137371904

> the level of productive forces and the degree of monopolistic concentration with the survival of the nation-state. By creating a larger area in which commodities, capital and labour circulate freely, it thereby releases industry from at least part of the fetters which Malthusian cartels, tariff walls and short-sighted economic nationalism had imposed upon it in the inter-war years. (Mandel, 1970, p.143)

It was envisaged that monetary union would eventually prefigure political federalism. The first experiment in monetary union, however, was a failure. International exchange rate volatility continued unabated after the formal abandonment of the Bretton Woods system in 1973. It was now possible for the US monetary authorities to pursue a policy of "benign neglect" and allow the dollar to progressively depreciate. By doing so, it was assumed that the US economy could recover its loss of export competitiveness in international markets (Parboni, 1981). This policy merely induced an inflationary upsurge and generated further instability in international financial markets. The European authorities attempted to stabilise intra-Community exchange rates with the introduction of a fixed exchange rate regime – the "snake in the tunnel" – which was designed to limit the degree of intra-Community exchange rate divergence and foster a more coherent means of exchange rate convergence. EMU was essentially a Franco-German accord. While the French authorities sought to stabilise the CAP, the Germans were more concerned about the destabilising impact of speculative capital inflows and their impact on domestic liquidity and their potential to generate excessive credit creation. At the same time, the secular appreciation of the DM had undermined Germany's export competitiveness. For the German authorities, EMU was an important means by which to preserve their export competitiveness within Europe and sterilise capital inflows by making the German mark a closer substitute for other EEC currencies. The adverse impact of an exchange rate appreciation would be offset by a superior anti-inflationary performance.

The debates between "economists" and "monetarists", which had preceded the official implementation of the Werner Report had reflected the divergent strategies advocated by the French and German authorities toward EMU. Represented by the Dutch and German experts, the "economists" advocated a gradualist strategy in which closer economic union would create the conditions for eventual monetary union. Their strategy implied a gradual convergence of economic policies between member countries with a rigorous anti-inflationary bias. The "monetarists", represented by French experts, on the other hand, advocated the

DOI: 10.1057/9781137371904

immediate realisation of monetary union with the irrevocable fixing of exchange rate parities and the pooling of reserves between the member countries. At stake in these debates was the issue of which country would incur the greatest burden of structural adjustment in the event of monetary union. This division reflected the conflicting imperatives of the deficit and surplus countries.

According to the seminal theory of optimum currency areas, monetary union implies that the surplus countries should pursue a reflationary policy in order to ease the adverse structural impact of higher unemployment experienced in the deficit countries (Mundell, 1961). In order to prevent the emergence of asymmetrical, county-specific shocks, the recycling of surpluses to the deficit countries was required, either in the form of providing additional credit or through an increase in the level of effective demand in the surplus countries. The ultimate solution to this problem of structural adjustment was identified by Mundell in terms of the increased mobility of labour. It was assumed that an asymmetrical shock would induce a labour migration from the deficit countries/regions to the surplus countries/regions. In the absence of a high degree of labour mobility and the unwillingness of the surplus countries/regions to increase their level of effective demand, these conflicting tendencies would become more acute under a fixed exchange rate regime or in the event of monetary union. Deprived of the ability to rely on exchange rate devaluations in order to adjust to an adverse economic shock, the deficit countries/regions would experience a more painful process of adjustment in terms of higher unemployment.

Given these divergent national economic trends, the issue of monetary union remained unresolved. With the onset of recession and the oil price shocks, the "snake in the tunnel" could no longer promote exchange rate stability and eventually succumbed to speculative attacks. The first experiment in EMU ended in failure. Indeed, EMU had devolved into an exclusive DM-zone. After the failure of the first experiment, it was considered highly unlikely that another attempt would be made. However, the renewed instability of the US dollar had generated a new wave of speculation in 1978. The steep slide in the dollar had threatened German export competitiveness and triggered another phase of financial and exchange rate instability. With the election of the Social Democratic government led by Chancellor Schmidt in Germany, the issue of EMU was resurrected despite powerful opposition from the Bundesbank. After the election of D'Estaing in France, Schmidt had found an accommodating ally in the revitalisation of the EMU project. This favourable political configuration

DOI: 10.1057/9781137371904

established the conditions for the birth of the European Monetary System. As the international economic environment improved after the cyclical recovery of 1982–83, intra-Community economic trends began to converge once again. Unlike its "snake" predecessor, the EMS was endowed with greater financial resources and exhibited a higher degree of flexibility in intra-ERM exchange rates. The most innovative feature of the EMS was the introduction of the Exchange Rate Mechanism, which was a central system of bilateral exchange rates in which the degree of fluctuation was limited to within (+/–) 2.25 per cent either side of parity. These bilateral rates were expressed in terms of the European Currency Unit, which was issued by the European Monetary Co-operation Fund and to which the central banks deposited 20 per cent of their gold and dollar reserves.

Germany emerged as the dominant country in an asymmetrical regime in which the DM performed the role of nominal exchange rate anchor for the EMS as a whole. While the German authorities were able to adjust their exchange rate policies through interest rate adjustments, the deficit countries increasingly resorted to the imposition of exchange rate and capital controls. Similarly, while the German authorities pursued a trade-off between economic growth and lower inflation, the deficit countries were compelled to sacrifice economic growth to achieve exchange rate stability. At the same time, the Bundesbank was staunchly opposed to the internationalisation of the German mark because of the inflationary risks involved. In contrast to the fixed exchange rate system under Bretton Woods in which the US economy provided an expansionary impetus for the international economy, Germany imparted a disinflationary impulse throughout the EMS zone. Although this process of "competitive disinflation" fostered a greater degree of exchange rate cohesion and discipline within the EMS with the convergence of national inflation rates, the ultimate costs were evident in terms of economic stagnation and rising unemployment, or what became known as the onset of "Eurosclerosis".

The internal asymmetrical dynamics of the EMS could no longer be accommodated as a vicious circle developed between the trade deficits in Italy and France, on the one hand, and the trade surpluses in Germany and the Netherlands, on the other hand. In the absence of a reflationary policy in Germany, the deficit countries were forced to rely on capital controls to maintain their respective exchange rate parities. Indeed, the impact of this exchange rate constraint on the ability of a deficit country to enact an expansionary programme was quite graphically portrayed in the failure of the French Socialist policies of "Keynesianism in one country" during the early 1980s. Germany therefore consolidated its hegemonic position in Europe in the 1980s by accumulating successive trade surpluses and accelerated the export of capital. This economic dominance was translated into the imposition of German ideological preferences in the form of quite severe disinflationary policies. In short, the EMS had evolved into an asymmetrical DM-zone that provided a sphere of exchange rate stability to which the majority of German exports were destined, while partially insulating the German economy from the destabilising impact of successive dollar devaluations after 1985. At the same time, the threat to Germany's export competitiveness within the EMS could be averted by limiting the degree of exchange rate fluctuations of the other member states within the Exchange Rate Mechanism. An analysis of the Maastricht blueprint for EMU revealed that the "convergence criteria" had institutionalised these German ideological preferences.

Germany's remorseless pursuit of competitive disinflation and domestic wage repression has reverberated within the EMU. This Kaleckian strategy of "monetary mercantilism" was characterised by low wage growth relative to the rate of productivity growth, which increased the relative share of profits and improved Germany's international export competitiveness (Kalecki, 1971). The accumulation of trade surpluses and the concomitant increase in aggregate profits created a rising surplus, which allowed Germany to export capital to the peripheral, deficit countries of Europe. To a large extent, these financial flows financed the balance of payments deficits of the peripheral countries and augmented their purchasing power (Cesaratto, 2012, p.12). In other words, the surpluses generated by Germany were absorbed by the peripheral, deficit countries. This virtuous circle, however, was only possible as long as the deficit countries were able to incur the main burden of adjustment via exchange rate devaluations. As soon as this exchange rate adjustment was ruled out under the EMS, the growing imbalances between the surplus and deficit countries threatened the internal cohesion of the currency zone.

It was the onset of the phenomena of "Eurosclerosis" from the mid-1970s onward that provided the catalyst for the Internal Market Programme in the mid-1980s. The relatively poor performance of the European capitalist economies in relation to their American and Japanese rivals had provoked considerable debate about the competitiveness and structural weaknesses of European industry. This lack of innovative and competitive dynamism would ostensibly be resolved with the implementation of a neoliberal programme, which involved the

DOI: 10.1057/9781137371904

dismantling of national regimes of regulation and protectionism. With a general shift to the political right during the 1980s and a crisis afflicting the social democratic alternative, the neoliberal programme gained the political ascendancy. Its proponents advocated the liberalisation of the European market through the removal of existing non-tariff barriers, the opening-up of public procurement policies and the liberalisation of capital markets. This strategy also implied the winding back of the power of organised labour and the deregulation of labour markets.

According to the influential Cecchini Report (1988), these ostensible "efficiency" gains would be secured through greater rationalisation and economies of scale, which would promote technological innovation and economic growth within a more uniform internal market enshrined by the 279 proposals that formed the basis of the Single European Act. The neoliberal strategy doubtless coincided and reflected the objectives of powerful transnational corporations based in Europe who sought to increase their penetration of the European market and improve their competitiveness against foreign rivals. The existing national regimes of accumulation were no longer considered to be compatible with the imperatives of globalisation. These national regimes of regulation, however, were not reproduced on the supranational level. In the absence of strategically powerful and coherent supranational state institutions of governance and regulation, the European market was quite vulnerable to asymmetrical, country-specific shocks.

The crisis of European capitalism appears to involve a breakdown of existing national modes of regulation. This study has identified three critical dimensions to the efficacy of the neoliberal strategy. First, is monetary union possible in the absence of a corresponding fiscal framework on a supranational level? Second, the problem of a European "social space" has emerged as national forms of labour market regulation and the whole plethora of wages, working conditions and social legislation has been subjected to the impersonal forces of the market. A European social space was therefore necessary in order to prevent the destructive phenomena of "social dumping" and the competitive bidding down of real wages between regions and countries in their attempts to attract an inflow of foreign investment. In this sense, the narrow imperatives of labour market deregulation and labour mobility, which informed the neoliberal strategy, merely reinforced this ubiquitous "race to the bottom". The third problem involved the regional consequences of this process of market liberalisation and monetary union. The evidence appears to suggest that these regional disparities have become more extreme.

DOI: 10.1057/9781137371904

The efficacy of the neoliberal strategy ultimately confronts the limits imposed by its own ideological opposition to the creation of more coherent forms of supranational regulation and governance. The theory of "negative integration" continues to inform the neoliberal design of EMU. Quite contrary to the optimistic projections made by the proponents of neoliberalism, this study contends that the liberal and deregulationist logic has merely accentuated regional disparities, eroded established social legislation and norms and severely limited the scope for traditional Keynesian policies of fiscal stabilisation and full employment. With the exception of Germany, the restoration of the competitive dynamism of European capitalism through the neoliberal strategy has failed to materialise. Indeed, the process of negative integration has already generated powerful centrifugal forces, which could act as a barrier to further progress toward European union. The recent eurozone debt crisis represents the culmination of these longstanding internal contradictions between the surplus and deficit poles of the currency zone. In its bare essentials, the euro remains a stateless currency. In the absence of fiscal federalism, the indebted peripheral countries are at the mercy of international bond markets. As a result, the internal cohesion of the eurozone rests upon the imposition of severe austerity measures on these peripheral, deficit countries. This vicious circle now threatens to degenerate into a depressive spiral reminiscent of the deflationary breakdown of the gold standard regime during the 1930s. In this critical context, the flawed Maaastricht design of the euro-system has only exacerbated these powerful asymmetrical forces, which now threaten the very survival of the European project in its existing form.

The possible break-up of the eurozone could set in motion the dormant though still powerful currents of nationalism and the revival of ethno-nationalist rivalries. A relapse into the syndrome of nationalist/imperialist rivalry which had engulfed the continent during the interwar years is quite possible. This scenario would presuppose an intensification of the current capitalist crisis and the collapse of the prevailing liberal-democratic forms of government. Although the objective conditions and the subjective forces for this kind of scenario appear to be relatively benign, nationalist political tendencies have already emerged in the wake of the current crisis. The growing ranks of the unemployed will doubtless provide a fertile breeding ground for the growth of these extremist nationalist forces. Scapegoats can be readily targeted with the presence of foreign workers. With the general shift to the political right,

DOI: 10.1057/9781137371904

racism has become the dominant ideological expression of this resurgent nationalism. In this sense, the recent Balkan conflict represents the most extreme manifestation of this ethnic/nationalist revival. The triumph of these forces could set in train the break-up of the post-war pan-European political project. At present, the likelihood of this disturbing scenario appears to be quite remote. A major economic catastrophe or war could, however, unleash these forces into the maelstrom of history.

The deep-seated structural crisis in Europe has resonated in the social and political spheres. With the relative demise of traditional social democratic policies and the ascendancy of the neoliberal economic paradigm, the post-war consensus based on "social market" policies has been seriously undermined. A single currency and a single market imply the supersession of national forms of state power and the creation of a supranational regime of governance. But the neoliberal strategy of negative integration does not propose to substitute these national forms of capitalist regulation on a supranational level. The political crisis is therefore an expression of the contending national/supranational forms of state power. Although European statehood would not necessarily abolish the existing system of national politics, the remorseless logic of globalisation has accentuated these social and regional disparities. Deprived of its traditional armour of sovereignty, nationalism could be re-activated to restore the primacy of the nation state and its monopoly over the issuing of fiat money. The restoration of the former regimes of state money would imply the eventual break-up of the eurozone and the possible onset of inter-state rivalries, reminiscent of the inter-war crisis. In this scenario, the outbreak of competitive devaluations and trade wars cannot be ruled out.

Another possible scenario involves the continuation and prolongation of German hegemony. Although the Franco-German axis still constitutes the pivot around which the process of European integration revolves, the German economy occupies the very core of Europe. This was evident not only in the relative size of the German economy but also in the strategic role performed by German neo-mercantilism and the export of capital from Germany as a result of the accumulation of persistent trade surpluses. German economic dominance was reflected in the politics of monetary union. The German mark emerged as the nominal exchange rate anchor for the EMS while German ideological preferences have prevailed in the creation of the ECB. Germany has been at the very core of Europe surrounded by a concentric circle of peripheral and semi-peripheral countries. In this configuration, the northern industrial regions constituted the centre to which the peripheral and semi-peripheral countries in the south and west gravitated. A third concentric circle also evolved with the newly emergent capitalist economies of eastern Europe. Given this new enlarged European sphere, the likelihood of European federalism appears difficult to accomplish. A loose confederation is the most likely outcome with Germany acting as the hegemonic centre. The ultimate question is whether the European Union will become a platform for future German economic expansion or whether Germany itself will form its own exclusive zone and break away from the enlarged EU.

A third scenario could be the "imagined community" of European federalism. Despite the ideals and aspirations of European federalists, the likelihood of European statehood appears as remote as ever. Indeed, much of the ostensible progress toward European federalism has been imbued with mythology. In the past, European countries have pursued an imperialist policy of territorial acquisition and expansion in order to resolve their domestic problems of markets and access to raw materials. One of the central aims of the post-war political settlement was to reconcile these inter-state rivalries within a pan-European framework. German militarism, in particular, could now be contained and to paraphrase Schuman, the post-war French Foreign Minister: "make war not only unthinkable but materially impossible". To this end, supranationalism has succeeded in fostering peace and prosperity within Western Europe. Indeed, as Milward has argued, post-war European union represented the rescue of the nation-state after the depredations of depression and war (Milward, 1992). European statehood could conceivably resolve some of the deep-seated and longstanding contradictions that have wreaked havoc in the wake of the recent debt crisis. Political union could represent a possible way out of the present impasse. The creation of a European Treasury endowed with a broad tax base, presided over by a European parliament with real legislative and executive powers, could provide the basis to re-launch a sustained Keynesian-type recovery through a European Marshall Plan. Unfortunately, neither the historical conditions, nor the political consensus exist to realise such an ambitious programme for recovery.

DOI: 10.1057/9781137371904

Bibliography

Aglietta M. (1982) *A Theory of Capitalist Regulation,* New Left Books, London.

—— (2012) "The European Vortex", *New Left Review,* Vol. 75, May/June, pp.33–61.

Al-Chalabi F.J. (1980) *OPEC and the International Oil Industry,* Oxford University Press, New York.

Arestis P. (1999) "The Independent European Bank: Keynesian Alternatives", *Working Paper* No. 274, The Jerome Levy Institute of Bard College, New York.

Arestis P. and Sawyer M. (2006a) (eds), *Alternative Perspectives in Economic Policies in the European Union,* Palgrave Macmillan, New York.

—— (2006b) "Macroeconomic Policy and the European Constitution", in P. Arestis and M. Sawyer (eds), *Alternative Perspectives in Economic Policies in the European Union,* Palgrave Macmillan, New York, pp.1–32.

—— (2007) "Can the Euro Area Play a Stabilizing Role in Balancing Global Imbalances?", in J. Bibow and A. Terzi (eds), *Euroland and the World Economy,* Palgrave Macmillan, New York, pp.53–75.

—— (2010a) "The Mediterranean Countries Are Being Condemned to High and Rising Unemployment", Blog: Re-Public: Re-Imagining Democracy; available at: http://www.re-public.gr/en/?p=2390 (accessed 20 July 2010).

—— (2010b) "The Problems of the Economic and Monetary Union: Is there any Escape?", *Journal of Economic Analysis,* Vol. 1, No. 1, pp.1–14.

—— (2011) "The Ongoing Euro Crisis" *Challenge*, Vol. 54, No. 6, Nov/Dec, pp.6–13.

—— (2012) "Can the Euro Survive the European Crisis?" in P. Arestis and M. Sawyer (eds) *The Euro Crisis*, Palgrave Macmillan, London, pp.1–21.

—— (2012) (eds) *The Euro Crisis*, Palgrave Macmillan, London.

Arestis P. and Chick V. (1995) (eds), *Finance, Development and Structural Change*, Edward Elgar, London.

Arestis P., McCauley K. and Sawyer M. (2001) "An Alternative Stability Pact for the European Union", *Cambridge Journal of Economics*, Vol. 25, No. 1, pp.113–30.

Artis M. and Lee N. (1994) (eds), *The Economics of the European Union*, Oxford University Press, New York.

Artis J. A. and Winkler B. (1997) "The Stability Pact: Safeguarding the Credibility of the European Central Bank", European University Institute, *Working Papers*, RCS No. 97/54, Florence.

Atkinson A.B. and Brunetta R. (1991) (eds), *Economics for the New Europe*, Macmillan & Co., London.

Bank of England Quarterly Bulletin (1990) "The Exchange Rate Mechanism in the European Monetary System", Vol. 30, No. 4, November, pp.479–81.

Bank for International Settlements (BIS) (2010) *Quarterly Review*, June, Basel.

Barba A. and Pivetti M. (2009) "Rising Household Debt: Its Causes and Macroeconomic Implications–A Long Period Analysis", *Cambridge Journal of Economics* Vol. 33, No. 3, pp.113–37.

Bellofiore R., Garibaldo F. and Halevi J. (2010) "The Global Crisis and the Crisis of Neomercantilism", in L. Panitch, G. Albo and V. Chibber (eds), *The Crisis This Time*, Merlin Press, London, pp.120–47.

Berger S. (1981) (ed.), *Organising Interests in Western Europe*, Cambridge University Press, London.

Bibow J. (2006) "How the Maastricht Regime Fosters Divergence As Well As Fragility", *Working Paper* No. 460, The Jerome Levy Institute of Bard College, New York.

—— (2007) "Global Imbalances, Bretton Woods II and Euroland's Role in All This", in J. Bibow and A. Terzi (eds), *Euroland and the World Economy*, Palgrave Macmillan, New York, pp.15–42.

DOI: 10.1057/9781137371904

—— (2012) "The Euro Debt Crisis and Germany's Euro Trilemma", *Working Paper* No. 721, May, The Jerome Levy Institute of Bard College, New York.

Bibow J. and Terzi A. (2007) (eds), *Euroland and the World Economy,* Palgrave Macmillan, New York.

Blackburn R. (2011) "Crisis 2.0", *New Left Review,* Vol. 72, Nov/Dec, pp.33–61.

Blanden-Hovell R. (1994) "The European Monetary System", in M. Artis and N. Lee (eds), *The Economics of the European Union,* Oxford University Press, New York, pp.328–45.

Block F. (1977) *Origins of Economic Disorder,* University of California Press, New York.

Boltho A. (1982) (ed.), *The European Economy,* Oxford University Press, New York.

—— (1993) "Western Europe's Economic Stagnation", *New Left Review,* Vol. 201, Sept/Oct, pp.60–75.

Bornstein S., Held D. and Krieger J. (1984) (eds), *The State in Capitalist Europe,* Sage Publishers, London.

Bramble T. (2009) "Crisis and Contradictions in the World Economy", *Journal of Australian Political Economy*, Vol. 64, pp.37–65.

Britton A. and Mayes D. (1992) *Achieving Monetary Union in Europe,* Sage Publishers, London.

Buiges T. and Goybet A. (1989) "The Community's Industrial Competitiveness and International Trade in Manufactured Products", in A. Jacquemin and A. Sapir (eds), *The European Internal Market,* Oxford University Press, New York, pp.227–47.

Bulmer P.J. and Paterson W. (1987) *The Federal Republic of Germany and the EC,* Allen & Unwin, London.

Camilleri P. (1989) "Beyond 1992: The Left and Europe", *New Left Review,* Vol. 175, pp.5–17.

Canzoneri M.B. and Rogers C.A. (1990) "Is the European Community an Optimal Currency Area?", *American Economic Review,* Vol. 80, No. 3, June, pp.419–33.

Carchedi G. (1997) "The EMU, Monetary Crises and the Single European Currency", *Capital & Class,* Vol. 63, pp.85–115.

—— (2001) *For Another Europe,* Verso, London.

Carr E. H. (1951) *The Twenty Years Crisis: 1919–39,* Macmillan & Co, London.

Cecchini P. (1988) *1992: The European Challenge,* Commission of the EC, Brussels.
Cesaratto S. (2010) "Europe, German Mercantilism and the Current Crisis", *Working Paper* No. 595, March, Quaderni Del Dipartimento Di Economia Politica, University of Sienna, Sienna, Italy.
—— (2012) "Controversial and Novel Features of the Eurozone Crisis as a Balance of Payments Crisis", *Working Paper,* No. 640, May, Quaderni Del Dipartimento Di Economia Politica, University of Sienna, Sienna, Italy.
Cesaratto S. and Stirati A. (2010) "Germany and the European and Global Crises", *International Journal of Political Economy,* Vol. 39, No. 4, pp.56–86.
Chevalier J.M. (1975) *The New Oil Stakes,* Allen Lane, London.
Christie R. (2012) "Banker Jitters as Deadline Looms", *Australian Financial Review,* March 3, p.16.
Coffey P. (1977) *Europe and Money,* Macmillan, London.
—— (1987) *The European Monetary System – Past, Present and Future,* Kluwer Academic Publishers, London.
Cohen B.J. (2011) *The Future of the Global Economy: The Euro Versus the Dollar,* Routledge, London & New York.
—— (2012) "The Future of the Euro: Let's Get Real", *Review of International Political Economy,* Vol. 19, No. 4, pp.689–700.
Committee for the Study of Economic and Monetary Union, (1989), *Report on Economic and Monetary Union in the EC* (The Delors Report), European Commission, Brussels.
Crotty J. (1983) "On Keynes and Capital Flight", *Journal of Economic Literature,* Vol. 21, No. 1, pp.59–65.
Daltrop A. (1992) *Politics and the European Community,* Longman Group, Ltd., Hong Kong.
De Cecco M. and Giovannini A. (1989) (eds), *A European Central Bank?,* Cambridge University Press, London.
De Grauwe P. (1992) *The Economics of Monetary Integration,* Oxford University Press, London.
—— (2010) "A Mechanism of Self-Destruction of the Eurozone," *CEPS Commentary,* (9 September 2010), Centre for European Policy Studies.
Deleplace G. and Nell E.J. (1996) (eds), *Money in Motion: The Post Keynesian and Circulation Approaches*, Macmillan, London.

DOI: 10.1057/9781137371904

Dumenil G. and Levy D. (1993) *The Economics of the Profit Rate: Competition, Crises and Historical Tendencies in Capitalism*, Edward Elgar, Aldershot, UK.

—— (2004) *Capital Resurgent: Roots of the Neoliberal Revolution.* Harvard University Press, Cambridge, MA.

Dyson K. (2008a) (ed.), *The Euro at 10: Europeanization, Power and Convergence*, Oxford University Press, Oxford & New York.

—— (2008b) "The First Decade: Credibility, Identity and Institutional 'Fuzziness'", in K. Dyson (ed.) *The Euro at 10: Europeanization, Power and Convergence*, Oxford University Press, Oxford & New York, pp.1–34.

Dyson K. and Featherstone K. (1999) *The Road to Maastricht,* Oxford University Press, Oxford.

Edwards J. and Fischer K. (1994) *Banks, Finance and Investment in Germany,* Cambridge University Press, London.

EEC Commission (1972) *Report to the Council and Commission on the Realisation by Stages of Economic and Monetary Union in the Community,* (The Werner Report), Brussels.

European Commission (2009) "The Economic Crisis in Europe: Causes, Consequences and Responses", *European Economy,* No. 7, Luxembourg.

Eichengreen B. (2011) *Exorbitant Privilege,* Oxford University Press, Oxford.

Eichengreen B. and Wyplosz C. (1998) "The Stability Pact: More Than a Minor Nuisance?", *Economic Policy,* Vol. 13, No. 26, pp.65–113.

Emerson M. (1984) (ed.), *Europe's Stagflation,* Clarendon Press, Oxford.

—— (1992) (ed.), *One Market, One Money,* Oxford University Press, New York.

Emmanuel A. (1972) *Unequal Exchange: A Study of the Imperialism of Trade,* Monthly Review Press, New York.

Farrell H. and Quiggin J. (2011) "How to Save the Euro and the EU: Reading Keynes in Brussels", *Foreign Affairs,* Vol. 9, No. 3, May/June, pp.96–103.

Feldstein M. (1997) "EMU and International Conflict", *Foreign Affairs,* Vol. 76, No. 6, November/December, pp.60–73.

Ferri P. (1990) *Prospects for the European Monetary System,* St. Martin's Press, New York.

Ferreiro J. and Serrano A. (2012) "The Economic Crisis in Spain: Contagion Effects and Distinctive Factors", in P. Arestis and

DOI: 10.1057/9781137371904

M. Sawyer (eds), *The Euro Crisis,* Palgrave Macmillan, London, pp.240–68.
Fields D. and Vernengo M. (2012) "Hegemonic Currencies During the Crisis: The Dollar Versus the Euro in a Cartalist Perspective", *Review of International Political Economy,* Vol. 19, No. 4, pp.1–20.
Finn D. (2011) "Ireland on the Turn?", *New Left Review,* 67, Jan/Feb, pp.5–39.
Fisher I. (1933) 'The Debt-Deflation Theory of Great Depressions', *Econometrica,* Vol 1, No. 3, pp.337–57.
Fitoussi J.P. (1993) (ed.), *Competitive Disinflation,* Oxford University Press, New York.
Frangakis M. and Huffschmid J. (2006) "EU Financial Integration: Constraints and Alternatives", in P. Arestis and M. Sawyer (eds), *Alternative Perspectives in Economic Policies in the European Union,* Palgrave Macmillan, New York, pp.37–85.
Frieden J.A. (1991) "Invested Interests: The Politics of National Economic Policies in a World of Global Finance", *International Organization,* Vol. 45, No. 4, pp.425–51.
Funabashi Y. (1988) *Managing the Dollar: From the Plaza to the Louvre,* Institute for International Economics, Washington.
Galbraith J. (2010) "The Great Crisis and the American Response", *Public Policy,* No. 112, The Jerome Levy Institute of Bard College, New York.
Garrett G. (1992) "International Co-operation and Institutional Choice: The European Community's Internal Market", *International Organization,* Vol. 46, No. 2, Spring, pp.533–60.
George S. (1991) *Politics and Policy in the European Community,* Oxford University Press, New York.
Gilpin R. (1975a) *US Power and the Multinational Corporation,* Macmillan & Co. Ltd, London.
—— (1975b) "Three Models of the Future", *International Organization,* Vol. 29, No. 1, December, pp.37–60.
—— (2000) *The Challenge of Global Capitalism,* Princeton University Press, New York.
Giovannini A. (1990) "The Transition to European Monetary Union", *Essays in International Finance,* No. 178, November, Princeton University, New Jersey.

DOI: 10.1057/9781137371904

Giovannini A. and Spaventa L. (1991) "Fiscal Rules in the EMU: A 'No Entry Clause'", in A. B. Atkinson and R. Brunetta (eds), *Economics for the New Europe*, Macmillan & Co., London, pp.99–126.

Gordon D.M. (1988) "The Global Economy: A New Edifice or Crumbling Foundation?", *New Left Review*, Vol. 168, March/April, pp.24–64.

Grahl J. and Teague P. (1989) "The Cost of Neo-Liberal Europe", *New Left Review*, Vol. 174, March/April, pp.33–50.

Gramsci A. (1971) *Selections from Prison Notebooks*, ed. Q. Hoare and G. Nowell Smith, Lawrence & Wishart, London.

Guerrieri P. and Padoan P. C. (1986) "Neo-Mercantilism and International Economic Stability", *International Organization*", Vol. 40, No. 1, pp.29–42.

—— (1989) (eds), *The Political Economy of European Integration*, Simon & Schuster, London.

Halevi J. (1995) "The EMS and the Bundesbank in Europe", in P. Arestis and V. Chick (eds), *Finance, Development and Structural Change*, Edward Elgar, London, pp.263–93.

Halevi J. and Kriesler P. (2004) "Stagnation and Economic Conflict in Europe", *International Journal of Political Economy*, Vol. 34, No. 2, pp.19–45.

Harvey D. (2006) *Spaces of Global Capitalism*, Verso, London & New York.

Hall P.A. (1984) "Patterns of Economic Policy: An Organizational Approach", in S. Bornstein, D. Held and J. Krieger (eds), *The State in Capitalist Europe*, Sage Publishers, London, pp.21–54.

Harrop J. (1989) *The Political Economy of Integration in the Community*, Edward Elgar Publishers, London.

Hein E., Truger A. and Van Treek T. (2012) "The European Financial and Economic Crisis: Alternative Solutions from a (Post-) Keynesian Perspective", in P. Arestis and M. Sawyer (eds) *The Euro Crisis*, Palgrave Macmillan, London, pp.35–79.

Henning Randall C. (1996) "Europe's Monetary Union and the United States", *Foreign Affairs*, Vol. 102, Spring, pp.83–101.

—— (1998) "Systemic Conflict and Regional Monetary Integration: The Case of Europe", *International Organization*, Vol. 52, No. 3, pp.537–73.

Holland S (1975) *The Socialist Challenge*, Quartet Books, London.

Iley R. A. and Lewis M.K. (2007), *Untangling the US Deficit*, Edward Elgar, Cheltenham, UK and Northampton, MA, USA.

DOI: 10.1057/9781137371904

Ingram J.C. (1973) "The Case for European Monetary Integration", *Essays in International Finance*, No. 98, April, Princeton University, New Jersey.
Jacquemin A. and Sapir A. (1989) (eds), *The European Internal Market*, Oxford University Press, New York.
James H. (2009) *The Creation and Destruction of Value: The Globalization Cycle*, Harvard University Press, Cambridge Massachusetts and London.
Jenkins R. (1978) *"Address on the European Monetary System" by the Rt. Hon. Roy Jenkins, President of the Commission of the European Communities, to the Degree Congregation, University of Essex. Essex, 20 July.*
Johnson H.G. and Swoboda A.K. (1973) (eds), *The Economics of Common Currencies*, Allen & Unwin, Ltd., London.
Kaldor M. (1978) *The Disintegrating West*, Allen Lane, London.
Kalecki M. (1943) "Political Aspects of Full Employment", *Political Quarterly*, Vol. 14, No. 4, pp.322–30.
—— (1954) *The Theory of Economic Dynamics*, Allen & Unwin, Ltd., London.
—— (1969) "On Foreign Trade and 'Domestic Exports'", in *Studies in the Theory of the Business Cycle: 1933–39*, Basil Blackwell, London, pp.16–25.
—— (1971) *Selected Essays on the Dynamics of the Capitalist Economy; 1933–70*, Cambridge University Press, London.
Karagiannis N. and Kondeas A. J. (2012) "The Greek Financial Crisis and the Developmental Path to Recovery: Lessons and Options", *Real World Economics Review*, Vol. 60, pp.54–72.
Keynes J. M. (1936) *The General Theory of Employment, Interest and Money*, Macmillan & Co, London.
Kindleberger C.P. (1984) *A Financial History of Western Europe*, Allen & Unwin, London.
Kitromolides Y. (2012) "The Irish Tragedy", in P. Arestis and M. Sawyer (eds), *The Euro Crisis*, Palgrave Macmillan, London, pp.159–95.
Kouvelakis C. (2011) "The Irish Cauldron", *New Left Review*, Vol. 72, Nov/Dec, pp.17–32.
Kriele M. (1977) "West Germany: The Dynamics of Expansion", *International Organization*, Vol. 31, No. 4, Autumn, pp.775–808.
Krippner G.R. (2005) "The Financialization of the American Economy", *Socio-Economic Review*, Vol. 3, No. 2, pp.173–208.

DOI: 10.1057/9781137371904

Krugman P. (2011) "Can Europe be Saved?", *New York Times*, (12 January 2011): available at: http://www.nytimes.com/2011/01/16/magazine/16Europe-html?scp=1&sq=Can%20Europe%20be%20saved?&st=cse (accessed 9 December 2011).

Kruse D.C. (1980) *Monetary Integration in Western Europe: EMU, EMS and Beyond*, Butterworths, USA.

Lapavitsas C. (2012) "For Its Own Sake, Greece Needs to Declare Default", *Sydney Morning Herald*, January 25.

Lapavitsas C., Kaltenbrunner A., Lindo D., Mitchell J., Painceira P. J., Pires J., Powell A., Senfors A. and Teles N. (2010) "Eurozone Crisis: Beggar Thyself and Thy Neighbour", Research in Money and Finance, *Occasional Report*, March, Department of Money and Finance, School of Oriental and African Studies (SOAS), University of London, London.

Lapavitsas C., Kaltenbrunner A., Lambrinidis D. G., Lindo D., Meadway J., Mitchell J., Painceira J.P., Pires J., Powell A., Senfors A. and Teles N. (2010) "The Eurozone Between Austerity and Default", Research in Money and Finance, *Occasional Report*, September, Department of Money and Finance, School of Oriental and African Studies (SOAS), University of London, London.

Lazonick W. and O'Sullivan M. (2000) "Maximizing Shareholder Value: A New Ideology for Corporate Governance", *Economy & Society*, Vol. 29, No. 1, pp.13–35.

Lead P. and Palacio-Vera A. (2012) "Portugal's Best Way Out of Economic Stagnation: Institutional Reform of the Euro Zone", in P. Arestis and M. Sawyer (eds) *The Euro Crisis*, Palgrave Macmillan, London, pp.195–234.

Lerner A. (1943) "Functional Finance and the Federal Deficit", *Social Research*, February, Vol. 10, No. 1/4, pp.38–51.

Llewellyn J. and Potter S. (1982) "Competitiveness and the Current Account", in A. Boltho (ed.), *The European Economy*, Oxford University Press, New York, pp.29–45.

Lucarelli, B. (2004a) "European Monetary Union: A Neoliberal Trojan Horse?", *Contributions to Political Economy*, Vol. 23, pp.81–93.

—— (2004b) *Monopoly Capitalism in Crisis*, Palgrave Macmillan, New York.

—— (2011) *The Economics of Financial Turbulence*, Edward Elgar, Cheltenham, UK.

DOI: 10.1057/9781137371904

—— (2011–12) "German Neo-Mercantilism and the European Sovereign Debt Crisis", *Journal of Post Keynesian Economics,* Vol. 34, No. 2, pp.205–25.

Magnifico G. (1971) "European Monetary Unification For Balanced Growth: A New Approach", *Essays in International Finance,* August, Princeton University Press, New Jersey.

Mandel E. (1970), *Europe vs America,* New Left Books, London.

Marsh D. (2009) *The Euro: The Politics of the New Global Currency,* Yale University Press, New Haven & London.

Masera R.S. (1987) "An Increasing Role for the ECU: A Character in Search of a Script", *Essays in International Finance,* No. 167, June, Princeton University, New Jersey.

Masera R.S. and Triffin R. (1984) (eds), *Europe's Money,* Clarendon Press, Oxford.

Mayer M. (1974) *The Bankers,* Weybridge & Tulley, New York.

McArthur J.L. (2011) "Mortgaging Irish Independence", *Monthly Review,* Vol. 62, No. 10, pp.40–49.

McKinnon R.I. (1963) "Optimum Currency Areas" *American Economic Review,* Vol. 53, No. 4, pp.717–25.

Micossi S. (1985) "The Intervention and Financing Mechanisms of the EMS and the Role of the ECU", *Banca Nazionale Del Lavoro,* Vol. 55, December, pp.327–45.

Milios J. and Sotiropoulos D.P. (2010) "Crisis of Greece or Crisis of the Euro?: A View from the European 'Periphery'", *Journal of Balkan and Near Eastern Studies,* Vol. 12, No. 3, September, pp.223–40.

Milward A.S. (1992) *The European Rescue of the Nation-State,* Routledge, London.

Minsky H.P. (1982) *Inflation, Recession and Economic Policy,* Harvester Press, London.

Moon B.E. (1982) "Exchange Rate System, Policy Distortions and the Maintenance of Trade Dependence", *International Organization,* Vol. 36, No. 4, pp.715–39.

Moravcsik A. (1991) "Negotiating the Single European Act: National Interests and Conventional Statecraft in the EC", *International Organization,* Vol. 45, No. 1, pp.19–56.

Mundell R.A. (1961) "A Theory of Optimum Currency Areas", *American Economic Review,* Vol. 51, No. 4, pp.657–65.

DOI: 10.1057/9781137371904

—— (1973) "Uncommon Arguments for Common Currencies", in H.G. Johnson and A.K. Swoboda (eds), *The Economics of Common Currencies*, Allen and Unwin, London, pp.114–32.
Myrdal G. (1957) *Economic Theory and Underdeveloped Regions*, Gerald Duckworth & Co., Ltd., London.
Nersisyan Y. and Wray L.R. (2010) "Deficit Hysteria Redux? Why We Should Stop Worrying About US Government Deficits", *Public Policy Brief*, No. 111, The Jerome Levy Institute of Bard College, New York.
Norfield T. (2012) "Derivatives and Capitalist Markets: The Speculative Heart of Capital", *Historical Materialism*, Vol. 20, No. 1, pp.103–32.
Nugent N. (1991) *The Government and Politics of the European Community*, Macmillan & Co., London.
OECD (1997) "Implementation of the Euro: Key Considerations from the International Business Perspective", 5 November, Paris.
Onaran O. (2010) "The Crisis of Capitalism in Europe, West and East", *Monthly Review*, October, Vol. 62, No. 5, pp.18–33.
Padoa-Schioppa T. (1988) (ed.), *Efficiency, Stability and Equity*, Oxford University Press, New York.
_____ (1984) *Money, Economic Policy and Europe*, Commission of the EC, Brussels.
_____ (1991) "Europe After 1992: Three Essays", *Essays in International Finance*, No. 182, May, Princeton University, New Jersey.
Palley T. (2010) "Europe's Debt Crisis and Keynes's Green Cheese Solution", available at: http://www.thomaspalley.com/?p=168 (accessed: 10 August 2010).
—— (2011) "The European Monetary Union Needs a Government Banker," *Challenge*, Vol. 54, No. 4, July/August, pp.5–21.
—— (2012) *From Financial Crisis to Stagnation*, Cambridge University Press, New York.
Panico C. (2010) "The Causes of the Debt Crisis in Europe and the Role of Regional Integration", Political Economy Research Institute (PERI), *Working Paper Series*, No. 234, September, University of Massachusetts, Amherst, MA.
Panitch L., Albo G. and Chibber V. (2010) (eds), *The Crisis This Time*, Merlin Press, London.
Papadimitrou D.B. and Wray R.L. (2012) "The Euroland's Original Sin", *Policy Note 2012/8*, Levy Economics Institute of Bard College, New York.

DOI: 10.1057/9781137371904

Papadimitriou D.B., Wray R.L. and Nersisyan Y. (2010) "Endgame for the Euro? Without Major Restructuring, The Eurozone is Doomed", *Public Policy Brief*, No. 113, The Jerome Levy Institute of Bard College, New York.

Parboni R. (1981) *The Dollar and Its Rivals*, New Left Books, London.

—— (1983) "Reflections on Williamsburg", *New Left Review*, Vol. 141, pp.72–78.

—— (1986) "The Dollar Weapon: From Nixon to Reagan", *New Left Review*, Vol. 158, pp.6–18.

Parguez A. and Seccarella M. (2000) "The Credit Theory of Money: The Monetary Circuit Approach", in J. Smithin (ed.), *What Is Money?*, Routledge, New York, pp.101–23.

Pasinetti L. (1998a) "European Union at the End of 1997: Who Is in the Public Finance 'Sustainability' Zone", *Banca Nazionale del Lavoro Quarterly Review*, Vol. 51, No. 204, March, pp.17–35.

—— (1998b) "The Myth (or Folly) of the 3% deficit/GDP Maastricht Parameter", *Cambridge Journal of Economics*, Vol. 22, No. 1, pp.103–16.

Pelagidis T. (2009) "Structural and Institutional Divergence in the European Union", *Challenge*, Vol. 52, No. 6, November/December, pp.101–13.

Petit P. (1989) "Expansionary Policies in a Restrictive World: The Case of France", in P. Guerrieri and P.C. Padoan (eds) *The Political Economy of European Integration*, Simon & Schuster, London, pp.231–62.

Petras J. and Rhodes R. (1976) "The Reconsolidation of US Hegemony", *New Left Review*, Vol. 1, No. 97, May–June, pp.36–53.

Pinder J. (1991) *European Community*, Oxford University Press, New York.

Pitellis C.N. (2012) "On PIIGS, GAFFS, and BRICS: An Insider-Outsider's Perspective on Structural and Institutional Foundations of the Greek Crisis", *Contributions to Political Economy*, Vol. 31, pp.77–89.

Pivetti M. (1998) "Monetary Versus Political Unification in Europe. On Maastricht as an Excuse in 'Vulgar' Political Economy", *Review of Political Economy*, Vol. 10, No. 1, pp.5–21.

Polychroniou C.J. (2012) "The Mediterranean Conundrum: The Link Between the State and the Macroeconomy, and the Disastrous Effects of the European Policy of Austerity", *Policy Brief*, No 124, Levy Economics Institute of Bard College, New York.

DOI: 10.1057/9781137371904

Roubini N. (2010) "Teaching PIIGS to Fly", available at: http://www.project-syndicate.org/commentary/roubini22/English/(accessed: 13 July 2010).

Ross G. (1992) "Confronting the New Europe", *New Left Review,* Vol. 191, pp.49–68.

Salvati M. (1981) "May 1968 and the Hot Autumn of 1969: The Responses of Two Ruling Classes", in S. Berger (ed.), *Organising Interests in Western Europe,* Cambridge University Press, London, pp.331–67.

Sandholtz W. (1993) "Choosing Union: Monetary Politics and Maastricht", *International Organization,* Vol. 47, No. 1, Winter, pp.1–39.

Sardoni C. and Wray L.R. (2006) "Monetary Policy Strategies of the European Central Bank and the Reserve Bank of the United States", *Journal of Post Keynesian Economics,* Vol. 28, No. 3, Spring, pp.451–72.

Seers D. and Ostrom K. (1983) (eds), *The Crisis of the European Regions,* Macmillan Press, London.

Seers D. and Vaitsos C. (1980) (eds), *Integration and Unequal Development: The Experience of the EEC,* Macmillan Press, London.

Shanks M. (1977) *European Social Policy, Today and Tomorrow,* Pergamon Press, Ltd., London.

Skidelsky R. (2000) *John Maynard Keynes: Fighting for Freedom, Vol. 3,* Viking, New York.

Smaghi L.B. (1993) "Progressing Towards European Monetary Integration: Selected Issues and Proposals", *Temi Di Discussione Del Servizio Studi,* Banca D'Italia, No. 187, January.

Smithin, J. N. (2000) (ed.), *What Is Money?*, Routledge, New York.

—— (2003) *Controversies in Monetary Economics*, Edward Elgar Publishing, Cheltenham, UK and Northampton, MA, USA.

Soros G. (2010) "The Crisis and the Euro", *New York Review of Books,* August 19.

—— (2012) *Financial Turmoil in Europe and the United States,* Public Affairs Books, New York.

Spaulding R.M. (1991) "German Trade Policy in Eastern Europe, 1890–1990: Preconditions for Applying Trade Leverage", *International Organization,* Vol. 45, No. 3, Summer, pp.343–68.

Spero J.E. (1977) *The Politics of International Economic Relations,* St. Martin's Press, Inc., London.

DOI: 10.1057/9781137371904

Index

DOI: 10.1057/9781137371904

DOI: 10.1057/9781137371904

DOI: 10.1057/9781137371904

DOI: 10.1057/9781137371904

DOI: 10.1057/9781137371904

DOI: 10.1057/9781137371904